HOW TO
MEMORIZE
THE
BIBLE

HOW TO
MEMORIZE
THE
BIBLE

ISAIAH HEMPE

Tzyon Press
www.tzyonpress.com
www.howtomemorizethebible.com

How to Memorize the Bible
Copyright © 2009 by Isaiah Hempe

ISBN – 978-0-9840725-0-7
Library of Congress Control Number: 2009929897
Printed in the United States of America
First Edition: 2009

Cover Design by Paul Maluccio

Published by:
Tzyon Press
P.O. Box 542131
Merritt Island, FL 32954-2131
www.tzyonpress.com

I will delight myself in thy statutes:

I will not forget thy word.

Psalm 119:16

I am grateful to my wife, family and friends who have encouraged me over the years that this book was taking shape. In particular, I wish to thank Dorothy Hibbard, Liz Hedleston, Carmeleta Riley, and Dean Spitzer for their support and useful suggestions. But most of all I wish to thank the LORD God, for the many blessings He has given me and His faithfulness and long-suffering mercy for all these years.

Table of Contents

Introduction

ave you ever wished you could memorize the Holy
Bible? Many people struggle in their attempt to
memorize even a few Bible verses, only to give up in
failure time and time again. Perhaps you already know a few
verses by heart. But have you ever had the desire to know
hundreds of verses, whole chapters, and even entire books of
the Bible by memory?

Do you think that it takes a specially gifted person to
accomplish that task? Well, it doesn't. Nearly anybody can
do it. You only need to understand and follow a few simple
fundamental principles.

If you are reading this book, then you probably already
have a desire to memorize the Bible. It is not a coincidence
that you are reading this right now.

Both Christians and Jews believe that the Bible is the inspired Word of God. Although they might disagree on certain books in the Bible and their interpretation, they generally agree that it is God's message to mankind, revealing Him to each of us individually. It is God's way of speaking directly to each of us and telling us, among other things, some basic information about why we are here, how we should live, and what we have to look forward to after this life.

A person can read the Bible every day and come away with something new each time. The Bible is not just a collection of ancient legends and stories, as its critics like to suggest. It is actually a channel to tap directly into the Spirit of God and let Him speak to each of us personally. There is a supernatural element to the Bible that separates it from any other book ever written.

Regular reading of the Bible is essential to those who believe in it. But actually memorizing the Word of God elevates a person to another level all together. It becomes a rock that we can build the foundation of our life upon. In fact, the Bible states very clearly:

> **Man shall not live by bread alone,**
> **but by every word**
> **that proceedeth out of the mouth of God.**
> Matt. 4:4; Deut. 8:3; Luke 4:4

Because when we memorize the Word of God, and write it upon our hearts (as God compels us to do in the Bible), it becomes a part of us as well. We draw even closer to God. It brings clarity to our lives because we begin to understand

God's will for us. It gives us wisdom of how to live a
successful life, how to properly relate to other people and how
to achieve true happiness. It shows us how to deal correctly
with any situation that may arise. It gives us comfort during
times of trouble and direction and hope to carry us forward.
And God promises in His Word that He will draw closer to
those who draw closer to him. So if you are reading this now,
I repeat, I believe that it is not simply a coincidence. It wasn't
until Moses actually turned toward the burning bush that God
spoke to him.

You've read the introduction. Like Moses, you've made
your own turn. Perhaps God is calling you now to take
you to another level of wisdom and faith that you've never
experienced before. I believe that this book will help you get
there.

Isaiah Hempe

How to Memorize

Before getting to the techniques of memorization, you should first understand some basic principles of how the human brain functions.

Research has shown that there are actually three kinds or levels of memory. They are known as **short-term**, **working**, and **long-term** memory.

Short-term memory involves such tasks as memorizing a series of numbers or somebody's name who you just met. It's been shown that most people have the ability to remember up to about seven bits of information for a short time. That's one of the reasons that telephone companies use seven-digit numbers. But they break up those seven numbers into two separate units to make them easier to remember. The additional area code is memorized as a separate unit. Most people memorize their social security number as three sections of numbers rather than as nine individual numbers.

When you are first learning something new, if you are distracted, you may forget a number or someone's name. But with practice and time you find yourself more able to recall them with little effort. Something has changed in your brain. Short term memory has changed into something else.

Working memory usually involves situations you are dealing with immediately. For example, you are preparing a meal and doing several things at once. You are boiling water on the stove, chopping vegetables on a block, and thawing meat in the sink. The phone rings and you run into the other room to get the remote. You remember that you are cooking the food when you pick up the phone, so you return to the kitchen and continue to prepare the meal as you are talking on the phone. You are doing several things at once and can remember that you are doing them all.

Then later on, during the evening, you are engaged with other events and your mind becomes concerned with those things. It has completely forgotten about the different aspects of preparing the meal. In fact, unless you intentionally try, you may never again recall that meal or the details of its preparation. At that time your brain was utilizing only the areas of working memory.

Working memory usually involves events that occur for a time span of about twenty minutes. When people are knocked unconscious with a concussion, they often lose memory of events that happened up to twenty minutes prior to their injury. Sometimes they lose even more memory than that. But after about twenty minutes or so, short-term and working memory items can begin to be transferred into the area of memory called **long-term** memory.

If you were to compare your brain to a computer, short-term and working memory exists in the random access memory (RAM) and is erased every time the computer is turned off. Both of these types of memory comprise your basic short-term memory.

Long-term memory is actually stored in a different part of the brain and works in a different way. It functions more like a hard drive on a computer. These are items or files that you can remember for a much longer duration. In fact, there is a theory that a person can retain these memories virtually their entire life. These memories may actually be permanent and you merely have to be prompted in a certain way to access them. This is why sometimes you have sudden recall or *flashbacks* of previous events or information from time to time. You thought that you had forgotten about them, but suddenly they come back to your memory. Actually, they never left. They were always there stored away somewhere in your memory banks. Just like on a computer hard drive.

This information consists of items like your name, date of birth, social security number and phone numbers that you use on a continual basis. More examples are the names of your family and closest friends along with the memories you've shared with them. Memories are often stored as visual images in your mind. Can you recall visual images in your mind of the house you lived in as a child and places where you played or travelled to? They may not be perfect images, but the images probably still exist. We can actually picture in our mind past events and even see ourselves engaged in those events. That type of memory is an entirely different aspect of memory study apart from the principals and techniques we will discuss in this book.

But it is important to understand how information is actually directed into long-term memory. There are two ways. One is **involuntary** and the other is **voluntary**.

The involuntary method we can't control. It occurs through trauma or strong emotional reaction. Have you ever heard someone say, "I'll never forget . . ."? They then proceed to tell you about a significant occurrence in their life that affected them in a powerful manner. We've all had experiences like that. For example, can you remember events at a funeral for a loved one, perhaps many years ago? Most baby-boomers can still recall where they were when they heard about President Kennedy's assassination. And pre-baby-boomers can still remember the events of when they heard about the Pearl Harbor attack. Yet these same people may find it hard to remember what they had for lunch three days earlier. This is a perfect example of short-term vs. long-term memory.

Some people are forever plagued by the terrible experience of a vicious physical attack or a personal tragedy that occurred in their distant past. The memory still haunts them, as much as they wish they could forget it. There is a reason they can't seem to forget memories like these. They are not supposed to!

Memories of traumatic events in our lives are part of the survival mechanism that we actually share with animals. This is the way animals learn things. Animals don't choose which things to remember in their lives. They remember things that are essential to their survival. They learn where they can find food or shelter and remember these things. They also remember anything that might have hurt them or endangered them in the past. And they avoid those things.

The **voluntary** way you channel information into your long-term memory you can control. It occurs through **repetition**! *Repetition is the key principle of all voluntary learning!* You make an effort to remember something when you repeat it over and over again. Just like learning to ride a bicycle. Each time you fall down, you get back up and keep trying. Once you've learned it, you never forget it. Actually the process of learning to ride a bicycle combines the first method of traumatic events, as well. When you fall and hurt yourself, you learn and remember how not to do that again.

Years ago I once had the good fortune to study Chinese Gung-Fu under a true master. He would teach us the traditional Chinese way. Every movement he showed us we would repeat at least a hundred times a day. Soon these movements became as natural to me as breathing.

This method of repetition is also the way we teach animals tricks that we want them to learn. Most every pet owner who has ever taught their pet a trick knows this principal. The pet learns the trick because you repeat it over and over again until they learn it. Usually you give the pet a reward for successfully completing the trick so this motivates them to remember. But without the reward and the repetition, the pet would never choose to voluntarily learn the trick.

Now how does all this apply to memorizing the Bible?

There are actually two levels to this process. One level is on a **practical** and scientifically proven basis. I'll discuss this one first. The second level is on a **supernatural** basis, which I'll discuss later.

The first level deals with the techniques of memorizing words and groups or lines of words. Actually, this level has been practiced for centuries by stage actors, who memorize long passages of their lines in a play.

I first learned this technique as a high school student studying drama and Shakespeare. At that time, in my youth, I had the dream of someday becoming a Shakespearian actor. I bought the complete works of Shakespeare and several recordings of Shakespearian plays performed by famous actors, like Richard Burton and Laurence Olivier. I would listen to the recordings over and over and study my book of plays. I was able to memorize all the verses of any character I wished. My drama teacher told me the secret to learning my lines. The secret was simply to learn – *one line at a time*!

This is the second key principle of the voluntary learning process called **decomposition**. You break large tasks into smaller ones. You don't begin by trying to memorize a page at a time or even a paragraph at a time. Instead you begin with just a word or two at a time. If you can memorize a single word, then you can memorize another word and then another. Until you know the entire line. Then you practice that line several times until you know it perfectly. And you can **speak** it perfectly.

You might have to repeat it 5, 10, or even 20 times or more. But eventually, your brain **will** remember it. Because when you make that attempt, by repetition, you actually force that information into the permanent storage part of the brain! That is simply how our brain operates. That is how we remember things that we feel are important to us.

Once you know that first line, you go on to the next line and practice that, by repetition, over and over until you have memorized that line. Then you add the second line to the first and repeat them together. When you are comfortable with both lines, then you add the next line. Then the next line and so on. Whatever you seek to memorize you learn one line at a time. When you add all the memorized lines together you employ the third and final phase of voluntary learning – **recomposition**.

These are the three principals of all voluntary learning – repetition, decomposition and recomposition. But the most important of these is **repetition**.

At first, the process might seem new and strange and it may take you awhile to even learn your first line. Maybe it will take quite a while to learn several lines that comprise a verse. But you will most surely find that as you practice this technique, and others I'll be showing you, it will actually become quite easy and you will find yourself learning more quickly as time goes on. The reason for this is that you will actually activate areas of your brain that were previously not used. There are theories that suggest we activate, or grow new neurons and alter synaptic junctions in our brains by forcing our brains to deal with information in this manner. Our brains actually become more efficient in processing and storing information.

But this is not unusual. This is the way your body operates in other areas, as well. Your muscles get stronger by lifting progressively heavier weights in the gym. You increase your oxygen uptake by consistent aerobic exercise. The more you practice and study chess and the more games you play, the stronger player you become.

The basic scientific principle here is *homeostasis*. The living organism, even on a cellular level, strives for an environment without stress. When stress is applied, it adapts to the situation by seeking to reduce and eliminate that stress. Muscles that are stressed with exercise become stronger and more efficient to reduce that stress. The brain, when stressed with certain information processing tasks, becomes more efficient in those tasks.

If you lift weights and eat properly, your muscles will get stronger naturally. If you practice *learning your lines*, your brain will automatically transfer that information into long-term memory. It's a basic biological process! In this book I'm going to show you what amounts to physical training for your brain to improve your memory.

But there is also a spiritual aspect that separates this memorization process from an ordinary actor's method.

As believers in the Bible, we know that there is a spiritual dimension to human beings that separates us from animals. The Bible tells us plainly that the first man, Adam, was created in the image of God. This does not mean that we actually resemble God physically, because God has no physical form that we can see or discern. But rather it means that we have many of the attributes of God. For example, we can speak things into existence. We can speak ideas, great plans, inspiration, comfort or even pain into existence and have it affect our own lives and the lives of others. How we use this great power of speech that God has given us is very important to our success or failure in life.

One of the reasons for memorizing the Word of God is to use it in our lives. The Word of God will always put us on the right path. It will point us in the best direction to go in our life journey in all situations. One of the best examples we find of this in the Bible is found in the books of Matthew and Luke when Jesus, after being baptized by John and receiving the Holy Spirit, goes off into the wilderness for forty days. There He is tempted by the devil. Each time, in response to the temptations, He quotes from the book of Deuteronomy. Jesus showed us how to apply the Word of God when adversity comes against us in life. In fact, Jesus did this all throughout His ministry on earth. That's one of the reasons that John described Jesus, in the first chapter of John, as the living Word of God. God spoke to us directly and showed us how to apply His Word in our lives.

One of the greatest and most comforting quotes from the Bible comes from Matthew 7.

Ask, and it shall be given you;
seek, and ye shall find;
knock, and it shall be opened unto you:

For every one that asketh receiveth;

and he that seeketh findeth;

and to him that knocketh it shall be opened.

Matthew 7:7-8

This is a promise from God that we can put our faith in. But does it mean that anything we ask for we will receive or anything that we seek we shall find? The answer is found in verse 11.

If ye then, being evil,

know how to give good gifts unto your children,

how much more shall your Father which is in heaven

give good things to them that ask him?

Matthew 7:11

The essential point here is that when we ask for "good things" God says He will give them to us. If we ask God to give us the gift of memorizing His Word, is this asking for a "good thing"? I certainly think so. I don't claim to be speaking for God, but I can tell you from personal experience that everyone I know who has fervently prayed to God for the gift of memorizing His Word and applied the methods found in this book has been successful.

Just how successful you are in your memory work will also be a function of your own discipline and determination. Study the techniques found in this book and then practice on some of the verses found in the Memory Book section. Follow the guidelines for creating your own Memory Book for your personal favorite verses. In a short time I am sure that you will begin memorizing more of the Bible than you probably ever thought possible.

E-Z Memory Format

One of the reasons why most people have a hard time memorizing the Bible is because their Bible is not conducive to memorization. Most people may only have one copy of the Bible and that copy has extremely small print which is very difficult even to read at all. And the verses are usually laid out in a multiple column format instead of one line at a time.

Here is an example of Psalm 23 from a Bible I own –

A Psalm of David

23 THE LORD is my shepherd; I shall not want.
2   He maketh me to lie down in green pastures: he leadeth me beside the still waters.
3   He restoreth my soul: he leadeth me in the paths
of righteousness for his name's sake.
4   Yea, though I walk through the valley of the
shadow of death, I will fear no evil: for thou art
with me; thy rod and thy staff they comfort me.
5   Thou preparest a table before me in the presence of mine enemies: thou anointest my head with
oil; my cup runneth over.
6   Surely goodness and mercy shall follow me all
the days of my life: and I will dwell in the house of
the LORD for ever.   *KJV*

Now what is wrong with this format? Practically everything! To begin with, the point size is so small I almost need a magnifying glass to even read it. My first advice to anyone buying a Bible is to *always* select Giant or Large Print point size.

Second, the type is laid out to fit the size of the columns. Even though the right side of the column is not justified, no thought appears to be given as to where the next line begins. There are even hyphenated words in the text which are annoying and usually only found when both sides of the columns are justified. Whether the columns are justified or not, these are common features in almost every Bible you will find and there is little you can do about it. Although as experienced readers, we are able to read and comprehend text formatted in this fashion, this format is not the best format for either reading comprehension or memorization. Its purpose is merely to fit as much text into the fewest number of pages possible. This is why it is necessary to create your own **Memory Book** for all the verses you wish to memorize. In a later chapter I'll show you how to do that.

But first, here is an example of a better format for the same Psalm laid out in a fashion more conducive for both reading comprehension and memorization. I call this the **E-Z-Memory Format.**

Psalm 23

The LORD is my shepherd; I shall not want.

He maketh me to lie down in green pastures:
he leadeth me beside the still waters.

He restoreth my soul:
he leadeth me in the paths of righteousness
for his name's sake.

Yea, though I walk
through the valley of the shadow of death,
I will fear no evil: for thou art with me;
thy rod and thy staff they comfort me.

Thou preparest a table before me
in the presence of mine enemies:
thou anointest my head with oil;
my cup runneth over.

Surely goodness and mercy shall follow me
all the days of my life:
and I will dwell in the house of the LORD for ever.

Notice how each line usually expresses only one or two thoughts. This is because each sentence is broken down into its fundamental components of phrases and clauses. An easy way to distinguish this is to look at where often the sentence breaks with a comma, semi-colon, or colon. In this manner you are viewing each thought individually within the sentence. This is actually an improved format for better comprehension as well as memorization. This is one of the basic ways that poetry is structured. In this manner, we can also see the beautiful poetic quality of the Bible.

When we memorize, we are not just memorizing words. We are memorizing groups of words that comprise thoughts. When these thoughts are laid out clearly line by line, the thought itself becomes much easier to discern and therefore, to remember. It is the thought and the words that we remember, not just the words. The words express the thought and therefore the two are linked together. One without the other is incomplete. It is when the thought, expressed by the words, becomes part of our memory that the thought becomes real to us.   All of our past is only real to us because of the memories we have of it. The memories give us the reality of the past. So when we put God's Word into our memory, that's when it truly becomes real to us. The more we put in, the more real it becomes.

And each line also reflects the tempo of delivery, in that a slight pause can be made at the end of a line. Practice on the delivery of your lines will develop your individual style of expression.

Also notice that although I have separated the verses, I have left out the verse numbers. If you are learning an entire Psalm, you do not need to remember the individual verse numbers and therefore they are no longer necessary.

In extended passages that involve several verses, I do not include verse numbers. This is because they are not important when learning extended verses or chapters at a time. They would actually just get in the way, because you do not repeat then when reciting the verses anyway. You simply know where the Bible passage begins.

When learning a single verse or a few verses together, then you may want to memorize the book, chapter and verse number. People have their own opinions on this. Some people prefer to memorize the book, chapter and verse number for every verse they know. It is certainly impressive to know hundreds of Bible verses along with their verse numbers. But it is also useful for reference if you want to look up that verse for some reason. You can remember where it is!

The principal here is that you first memorize the location information – then the verse. For example:

Genesis 1:1

In the beginning God created the heaven and the earth.

When we learn this verse, we first memorize –

Genesis 1:1

Then we memorize –

In the beginning God created the heaven and the earth.

But if we were going to memorize an extended portion or even the entire chapter of Genesis 1, we would memorize the book and chapter, then the text line-by-line without regard for verse numbers. In this case we could begin with –

Genesis 1

In the beginning God created the heaven and the earth.

And the earth was without form, and void;
and darkness was upon the face of the deep.
And the spirit of God moved upon the face of the waters.

And God said, Let there be light: and there was light.

And God saw the light, that it was good:
and God divided the light from the darkness.

And God called the light Day,
and the darkness he called Night.
And the evening and the morning were the first day.

Each time we repeat the verse, verses or chapter, we always begin with the location, then the verse. That way we tie the two together in our memory files.

This method of limiting location information to only the book and chapter can also apply to individual verse memorization, as well. It's much easier to remember the basic location of a book and chapter without regard for the actual verse number. This is because we only have to memorize one (1) number each time!

For example, let's say we want to memorize the Aaronic blessing found in the book of Numbers. It actually begins at Numbers 6:24 and carries through to 6:26. Instead we could memorize it in this fashion:

Numbers 6

The LORD bless thee, and keep thee:

The LORD make his face shine upon thee,
and be gracious unto thee:

The LORD lift up his countenance upon thee,
and give thee peace.

The point here is that you still have the basic location information for reference. The actual verse location is really not that important because if you want to look it up, go to Numbers 6 and you'll find it. The important information is the text itself. The location information is really secondary.

You will find if you limit all your location reference to the book and chapter information, your verse memorization will be much easier.

Something to remember is that the original Bible did not include chapter or verse numbers. That system of organization was first created during the middle ages when the Bible began being translated into various European languages and printed. The standard chapter divisions, which are still used today, were created by Stephen Langton in 1551. The first Bible to divide the text into verses was the Geneva Bible in 1560. A French printer, Robert Estienne, is credited for the verse numberings that we still retain to this day. These are remarkable achievements of Christians who have sought to preserve the Holy Bible that is still the most popular book of all time.

Keep in mind that chapter and verse numbers serve to provide organization to the Bible. The important thing is the message, not necessarily the numbering of its organization. So if you never remember a single chapter or verse number, it's not that important anyway! But you can always reference any verse from the Bible the way Jesus usually did it and simply say, "It is written . . ."

Line Memorization

Remember that the basic procedure for line memorization is to learn line-by-line. Here is a technique that many have found useful.

After you have selected the verses that you wish to memorize, take a blank piece of paper, like an index card, and cover all the text except the first line. Then totally focus on only that line. Repeat it several times, out loud, to yourself. Then close your eyes and repeat it again a few times. Dwell on it in your mind to yourself for awhile. Try to completely understand its essence and meaning. Then open your eyes and without looking at the text, repeat it again a few times. When you have it, go onto the next line and repeat the procedure. When you have the second line, repeat the first line and add the second line to it. Then repeat the two lines together, with your eyes closed a few times. Dwell on them together to yourself. Again try to understand their combined essence and meaning. They are now becoming inseparable in your mind.

When you are ready, then go onto the next line and repeat the procedure.

At first, you might become tired after only a few lines and want to quit for the day. This type of focus and concentration can be mentally exhausting when you are just starting and inexperienced. But don't be discouraged. That's okay. With time and practice, just as in any exercise, your stamina will increase. Soon you won't tire as quickly and your mental endurance will increase so that the entire process is not difficult. Instead you will find it natural and relaxing. Because your mind will adapt to the task you have given it.

Imagine if you only learned one verse a day. That's not hard at all. But after a year you would know 365 verses! That's quite an achievement. Very few people can claim that ability. Then imagine if you only learned two verses a day. Or only three verses a day. You can see the point. With time, you will have memorized more of the Bible than you probably ever dreamed you could. Yet it would only take a few minutes a day of practice.

The more you practice this, the easier it will be to memorize your lines. You'll soon be able to learn multiple verses at every sitting. The key is consistency of effort and the focus and desire to continually advance in your memory work.

Here are some additional techniques to make your line memorization easier.

Suppose you want to memorize Psalm 19. It's a beautiful Psalm that can be recited as a daily prayer. But let's break it down line-by-line to see some specific techniques of memorization. We'll be using the King James Version (KJV). The first verse begins -

Psalm 19

The heavens declare the glory of God;
and the firmament sheweth* his handiwork. *(showeth)

Let's look at each line individually. These are simple declarative sentences. They are arranged in the basic order of subject, verb, and object. In the first sentence, the subject is "heavens". In the second sentence the subject is "firmament". As an interesting side-note, in the original Hebrew the second sentence actually reads more like, "and the work of his hands tells the firmament." Also notice that I suggested substituting the word "showeth" instead of its original spelling in the KJV of "sheweth". That just makes it easier to understand but doesn't change the meaning at all. A later chapter will discuss the pros and cons of the KJV as your source translation in more detail.

In the first sentence the word "heavens" is contrasted with "firmament" in the second sentence. It's like saying, "heaven and earth". So when you think of these two sentences together, you make a kind of mental note to yourself of that contrast to make it easier to remember the two lines together. You think heaven and earth or heaven and firmament. The first line continues . . . "declare the glory of God." "Glory of God" is a familiar phrase and can be remembered like that. The two words "glory" and "God" both begin with the letter "g". Remembering the first letter of key words is another useful technique for enhancing memory.   I'll be showing you more examples of this.

The second and third verses continue –

Day unto day uttereth speech,
and night unto night sheweth* knowledge.

There is no speech nor language,
where their voice is not heard.

In the first line here, you have the contrast of "day unto day" with "night unto night". Again, you make a mental note of that contrast. If you can remember "day unto day" the opposite of that would be "night unto night". Do you see the point? These little mental notes are not something to dwell upon but rather serve as a prompt for your memory when first learning the verse. Later on as the verse becomes part of your permanent memory files, the words will just flow naturally and the need of the prompt will rarely be necessary unless you let yourself go for awhile without reciting the verse and you need the prompt to refresh your memory.

Also notice how the word "speech" is repeated in the third line. This is another point to make a mental note of. The word "speech" leads you off and is basically repeated again with the word "language". Then it's followed with the word "voice". This repetition of similar words is quite common in Hebrew poetry and so much of the Bible is written in this poetic style. To enhance your understanding of the Bible, a separate chapter will explain in more detail the various elements that make up Hebrew poetry.

The next verse reads –

Their line is gone out through all the earth,
and their words to the end of the world.
In them hath he set a tabernacle for the sun,

In this verse the first two lines are **synonymous**. The second line is very similar to the first line, but repeats it in another way. This is one of the most common elements of Hebrew poetry called **parallelism**. There are basically six types of parallelism found in Biblical poetry which we'll cover in that later chapter.

But with regard to your memory techniques, after you have memorized the first line, you make a mental note of the synonymous aspect of line two. In the second line, "world" is used in place of "earth". And "words" also begins with the same letter as "world". So we have the letter **w** twice in this line. The final line contrasts with the first two in that it mentions the "sun". Try to grasp the image in your mind that the entire verse is trying to describe. And remember the unique word "tabernacle" which is basically a tent-like enclosure.

The next verse reads –

Which is as a bridegroom coming out of his chamber,
and rejoiceth as a strong man to run a race.

One of the great qualities of the KJV is the beautiful poetic choice of words that the translators used. Mark Twain once said, in commenting about the craft of writing, that the difference between the right word and almost the right word is like the difference between lightning and the lightning-bug! Time and time again I find that exactly the right word seems to be chosen in the KJV.

Repeated sounds draw attention in verse and add a poetic effect. This is not to be confused with words that rhyme. The effect is usually achieved by using words that begin with the same letter, i.e. "**c**oming out of his **c**hamber" and "**r**ejoiceth as a **s**trong man to **r**un a **r**ace."

It is a subtle feature which is most notable when spoken aloud. You will find it throughout the KJV, so obviously the translators appeared to be trying to achieve that effect. When read in the original Hebrew, the first sentence could have been translated like – "And he as a bridegroom goes out from his canopy". "Coming out of his chamber" has essentially the same meaning, but the English words chosen to represent the original Hebrew just seem to fit together more beautifully.

Let's drop down to verses 7, 8, and 9 to see another memory technique. These verses read –

The _torah_* of the LORD is perfect, converting the soul: *(law) the testimony of the LORD is sure, making wise the simple.

The statutes of the LORD are right, rejoicing the heart:

the commandment of the LORD is pure, enlightening the eyes.

The fear of the LORD is clean, enduring for ever:
the judgments of the LORD are true and righteous altogether.

The first thing you might notice is the word *"torah"*. In the KJV the word used is "law".

But *torah* is actually the original Hebrew word that has been translated into "law". In a later chapter I'll explain the reason I prefer the original Hebrew word of *torah* in all my memory work of the Old Testament.

Notice also what I've done in each sentence. I've underlined certain letters. All six lines are synonymous in structure which can be confusing at first to memorize and not get them mixed up. But here is how we can solve that problem. We apply a principle of mnemonics, which is the art of improving memory by various formulas. In this case we use word associations.

We remember that the subjects in the first two sentences begin with "t". Among other things, Torah is the traditional Jewish term for the first five books in the Bible. Because the Torah comes first in the Bible, it is easy to remember as the first subject. Then we just remember "t –t – s – c" as the order of the words for the first four lines. You should get very familiar with words like testimony, statute, commandment, fear and judgment because they are important and frequent words throughout the Bible. In the last two lines we see "fear" contrasted with "judgments". Since we are all to be judged in the end, this word seems fitting to be last.

I rarely use mnemonic formulas for Bible memorization. In special cases such as this one, they can be useful. But rather through repetition and practice the lines and verses will become part of your permanent memory. As you practice these techniques and utilize them in your memory work, you will find that they will become natural and instinctive to you. These are logical methods that will help you organize and structure your thinking. Some have been used for thousands of years by stage actors who memorize entire plays. But they can also easily be applied to memorizing extended text from the Bible.

But ultimately it is the power of God which will give you the ability to memorize His Word. Draw upon God's power in all your efforts. Each time before you begin your memory work, spend a few moments praying to God for His blessings and guidance. Then you are sure to succeed.

Creating Your Memory Book

Once you have selected the Bible verses that you wish to memorize, rather than trying to memorize them directly from your own Bible, the best way is to create your own **Memory Book** for all your memory work. This way you can lay out the text using the **E-Z Memory Format** and you have an arrangement of all the verses you have memorized. You can see your progress as your collection grows and you have a handy reference source to refer to if needed.

To get you started, there is an extensive Memory Book collection at the end of this book. But for any other verses that you wish to memorize, you'll want to construct your own individual Memory Book.

There are two ways to create your own Memory Book – the old fashioned way and the modern way.

The old fashioned way is to write everything by hand that you want to memorize. It is an easy and inexpensive way to get started. To begin, buy a medium-sized spiral bound notebook. It should have at least 30 lines per page, the more the better.

Perhaps you want to memorize the Lord's Prayer found in Matthew 6:9-13. It is one of the most beautiful and inspirational prayers ever created. Using a good quality pen, carefully *print* all the verses on one page. Don't write them or scribble them – print them as clearly as you can. This is important. You want the passage in your Memory Book to be clear and easy to read. It is best to combine upper and lower case letters just as it appears in the text you are copying. Imagine yourself as an ancient scribe hand-printing sacred text. Actually, you are a modern scribe hand-printing sacred text. Anytime you actually write down the Word of God, it is a serious matter. Do it with reverence and care. Here is an example.

Matthew 6:9-13

Our Father which art in heaven, Hallowed be thy name.

Thy kingdom come. Thy will be done in earth,
as it is in heaven.

Give us this day our daily bread.

And forgive us our debts, as we forgive our debtors.

And lead us not into temptation,
but deliver us from evil:
For thine is the kingdom, and the power, and the glory, for ever.
Amen.

At first you might have no particular order for your various verses. This is fine. Just write them down in any order you choose at first. But as time goes by and you begin learning more and more verses, you will probably wish to organize your Memory Book in a different fashion. For example, you might want to have all the Psalms in one section, all the Proverbs in another, all the passages of individual books in their own sections. With time and practice, you'll find an arrangement order that suits you. At some point you may decide to start all over again and re-organize your entire book. Believe me, I've been through that many times myself.

But that leads us into the more modern way of creating your Memory Book; using your computer. With this method, you use your word processing program to type out whatever verses you wish to memorize. Save them on files you select. Then print them out and put them together in a binder. This way any re-organizing is easy because you can simply rearrange the already printed pages.

Here is something to keep in mind. Your Memory Book is merely a tool to facilitate your memory work. It is a useful tool when you are first beginning to memorize your personal collection of Bible verses and chapters. It helps as a quick reference source when you want to refresh your memory. It also gives you a visual measure of your progress.

But when you get to the higher levels of memory ability, you may find that a personal Memory Book is no longer even necessary! The Bible itself becomes your Memory Book!

Some students of mine who have excelled to the highest levels of memory ability no longer even bother writing down their verses separately. They simply read the text right from their Bible and memorize it. They have trained their eyes to see the text in the **E-Z Memory Format** no matter how it is laid out. Some even claim they can sometimes see the text in their mind and they read it from that image they have. Their minds have evolved to a level approaching a photographic memory capability. They have adapted their memory in a special way. Whether it is a normal biological process or a divine gift, I do not know. I only know that it happens. And it is wonderful when it does. So keep that in mind for the future.

But stay with your Memory Book at first. Learn and practice the E-Z Memory Format method of laying out your text. Then see what the future has in store for you.

Beginning Your Collection

Now you have learned the basic principles of memorization. Let's put them to work in beginning your memory collection. You might be asking yourself, "Where shall I begin?" The answer to that question will be entirely up to you.

Each individual will have their own parts of the Bible that they are drawn to. Some people begin by learning a few Psalms that they love. Some people want to learn individual verses that provide them wisdom, comfort or a foundation to their own theological doctrines. My best advice is to pray for the answer and truly seek guidance from the Holy Spirit in everything you do with regard to your memory work. The Word of God is not something to take lightly. Rather it is something to always treat with the upmost respect and reverence. Whichever way the Holy Spirit leads you will be the right path for you.

But, whenever people ask me where they should begin, I usually want to ask them a very simple question first. "Have you read the entire Bible at least one time cover-to-cover?" I'm amazed at how many people tell me that they have not. If we are to believe in something, we certainly need to know what it is we believe in. I always tell people that in addition to their memory work, they also set aside some time to read the Bible in its entirety. It will be an enormous blessing to you and greatly increase your understanding of your faith and how to effectively apply it to your life. Read it in exactly the order it is arranged. Start in Genesis and don't stop until the last chapter of Revelation. Just read it one time completely to become familiar with it and comprehend it as one unified message to us from God. Afterwards, you might want to go back and combine it with some good commentary. I'm not going to recommend any particular commentary, because that is beyond the scope of this book. My purpose is not to direct people toward any particular viewpoint. But the more you know about the Bible, the better you will be able to select those portions you find most useful for yourself.

Don't be discouraged if you don't immediately begin by learning numerous verses at once. In fact, I recommend starting by learning just a single verse or even a single line your first day. Start small and work your way up. Delight yourself in your memory work and make it a pleasant experience rather than some sort of contest. You are not competing with anyone so don't concern yourself if your initial progress seems slow at first. Many people find it that way because it takes time for our brain to adapt to the new tasks we are giving it. The key is consistency of effort, discipline and confidence. As the days go by you will be pleasantly surprised at how easier and easier it all becomes for you.

Let's say, for example, that you want to begin with Psalm 1. It's a wonderful Psalm and one of my personal favorites. In my opinion, every Christian and Jew should know this Psalm by heart.

I've included this Psalm in the Memory Book at the end of this book. Here is the first verse.

Psalm 1

Blessed is the man that walketh not
in the counsel of the ungodly,
nor standeth in the way of sinners,
nor sitteth in the seat of the scornful.

Practice the verse one line at a time until you have that line down perfectly, then go on to the next line and practice that one. When you have that one, practice the two together until you have them down perfectly, and then repeat them with the next line. After you have the four lines, stop there for the day. That was your first verse. Now spend the rest of the day going about your normal activities, but with one simple addition. You will practice the verse all throughout the day to yourself whenever you get the chance. Take this book with you in case you need a little reminder of anything or copy the verse down in your own Memory Book.

For example, when you drive to work you practice your verse. When you're walking to your job or office, you're practicing your verse. When you have some free time to yourself at any moment, you're practicing your verse. You're practicing your verse all throughout the day. When you drive home and later that night, you're practicing your verse. By the end of that first day, you will know that verse! And you'll know that verse for the rest of your life if you simply repeat it at least once every day. It's that easy.

The next morning you write down the next verse and learn that one. Then you spend the day repeating the two verses together. At first just stick to learning one new verse a day for awhile. Pretty soon, that will seem too easy and you'll want to learn more than one verse a day. In fact, after awhile you'll probably be taking time out during the day to learn even more verses.

When you've finished the entire Psalm, practice it every day whenever you get the chance. Make it a principle that whenever you start a Psalm you must always finish it. It can never be left unfinished. In that way your brain will store and organize your memory work more efficiently. Try to do this with whatever you memorize, whether it's a collection of verses or entire chapters of scripture. Once you have learned something completely, then whatever you start must always be finished. Nothing is left undone.

Obviously you are going to find after awhile that it takes quite some time to actually repeat all the verses that you've memorized. Try timing how long it takes. When it takes you over an hour to recite all your verses you will know that you are making real progress! It takes approximately 75 hours to recite the entire King James Bible. That's if you're speaking at a normal pace the way an actor might record it.

Henry H. Halley, the author of *Halley's Bible Handbook*, had remarkable memory ability. He could recite from memory about one third of the entire Bible; over 25 hours of nothing but scripture, including extended passages from every book in the Bible. Few people will ever approach that level of ability. But you will be amazed at how much of the Bible you will be able to memorize if you consistently practice.

I'm sure that you've heard the saying, "If you don't use it, you'll lose it." One way to assure that you retain your collection of verses is to repeat them on a regular basis.

The actual amount of time each day you devote to memorizing new verses can be quite short. Anywhere from 10 to 30 minutes is plenty of time. But you can practice the verses you already know for as long as you like throughout the day. Here is the secret to never forgetting the verses that you've memorized – *all you need to do is repeat each verse that you've memorized **once** each day, and you will remember them the rest of your life.* You'll never forget them, because you repeated them at least once each day. It's as simple as that!

When are some good times to practice your verses? Anytime you're alone is always a good time. Driving to and from work is a great time. Try turning off the radio and the CD player and just take that time to recite every verse you've memorized to that point. Of course, a word of caution; don't get so absorbed in your verses that you aren't paying attention to your driving!

In the morning when you first wake up and just before going to bed are other times that are ideal for practicing your memory work. In fact that concept is part of the *Shema*, the fundamental statement of faith in Judaism that every observant Jew repeats when they retire and when they arise. Jesus must have repeated the *Shema* every evening and every morning this way, because it's actually one of the 613 commandments in Judaism. You have the Word of God on your lips as you go to sleep and when you first arise.

A good practice is to develop a pattern of repetition for your verses. For example, you could recite all the Psalms and Proverbs that you know together as a group. Let's say that you've memorized extensive verses or even whole chapters from the Book of Isaiah or the Book of Matthew. You could start with the verses at the earliest parts of each book and continue through to the ones toward the end of each book. If you were to recite these for an audience, they would get a wonderful sample of the words from each of those books in your arrangement.

If you memorize a large number of Psalms, don't fall into the habit of always repeating them in the same order. It's better to mix up the order of repetition so that your mind does not classify them together into one large memory unit. The individual Psalms will be the memory units in your mind.

When memorizing entire chapters or extended parts of chapters, again, the chapter should be the individual memory unit in your mind. So mix these up as you practice them, as well.

In the area of individual verse memorization, there is wide latitude for creativity. With time you will most surely find your own individual way of organizing your own verse selections. But here is a suggestion to start with that can get you going.

One of my favorite arrangements is what I call a **memory chain**. I recite a series of verses that are connected in a fashion that a main word ending one verse is in the beginning of another verse. Here is an example.

Luke 4:4

And Jesus answered him, saying,
It is written, That man shall not live by bread alone,
but by every <u>word</u> of God.

Prov. 30:5

Every <u>word </u>of God is pure:
he is a shield unto them that put their <u>trust</u> in him.

Prov. 3:5-7

<u>Trust</u> in the LORD with all thine heart;
and lean not unto thine own understanding.
In all thy ways acknowledge him,
and he shall direct thy paths.
Be not wise in thine own eyes:
<u>fear</u> the LORD, and depart from evil.

Prov. 9:10

The <u>fear</u> of the LORD is the beginning of <u>wisdom</u>:
and the <u>knowledge</u> of the holy is <u>understanding</u>.

Prov. 2:6-7

For the LORD giveth <u>wisdom</u>:
out of his mouth cometh <u>knowledge</u> and <u>understanding</u>.
He layeth up sound wisdom for the righteous:
he is a buckler to them that <u>walk</u> uprightly.

Psalm 119:1

Blessed are the undefiled in the way,
who <u>walk</u> in the <u>law*</u> of the LORD.   *(torah)*

Isaiah 2:3

For out of Zion shall go forth the <u>law*</u>,   *(torah)*
and the <u>word</u> of the LORD from Jerusalem.

John 1:1-2

In the beginning was the <u>Word</u>,
and the Word was with God, and the Word was God.
The same was in the beginning with God.

You see how you could carry a memory chain on indefinitely. This is also a great exercise in recalling verses based upon some key word that serves as a memory prompt. The more verses you memorize, the more you will be able to draw upon. But memorizing along the lines of a memory chain is also a great way to increase the number of verses you memorize and give them a useful arrangement in your mind.

Try starting a memory chain and add a new verse every day for a month. Then after the month is up, don't stop. Keep adding a new verse each day and see how far you can go.

With a memory chain, I don't bother with the location information of book, chapter and verse when reciting it. That just gets in the way and breaks up the flow of the message. I included it here just for your reference. But if you want to include it, that's up to you.

Another variation of a memory chain is combining a series of verses around a single theme. This is a great way to utilize the Word of God in your life to promote positive change.

Suppose you find that you have a personal problem with speaking things that you regret afterwards. You want to make a change and be more careful in the things you speak to people. So you select a series of verses which deal with speech and connect them together and recite them periodically throughout the day and especially before you have something important to say to anyone else. Here is an example:

Psalm 19:14

Let the <u>words</u> of my <u>mouth</u>,
and the meditation of my heart,
be acceptable in thy sight, O LORD,
my strength, and my redeemer.

Psalm 34:13

Keep thy <u>tongue</u> from evil,
and thy <u>lips</u> from speaking guile.

Psalm 39:1

I said, I will take heed to my ways,
that I sin not with my <u>tongue</u>:
I will keep my <u>mouth</u> with a bridle,
while the wicked is before me.

Psalm 49:3

My <u>mouth</u> shall speak of wisdom;
and the meditation of my heart shall be of understanding.

Psalm 34:1

I will bless the LORD at all times:
his praise shall continually be in my <u>mouth</u>.

Psalm 139:4

For there is not a <u>word</u> in my <u>tongue</u>,
but, lo, O LORD, thou knowest it altogether.

Prov. 18:21

Death and life are in the power of the <u>tongue</u>:
and they that love it shall eat the fruit thereof.

Memory chains that follow a single theme do not need to be very long. Their purpose is function rather than quantity. Even a single verse is sufficient if it accomplishes the task you are seeking.

Finally, let's discuss the time and place for your study. Where and when you do your memory practice is a matter of personal choice. Personally, I prefer to do my study in the early morning, shortly after awakening. In the still quiet of the morning, at the beginning of the day, is such a wonderful time to spend with the LORD God who created us. Many find that early in the morning is a special time they want to set aside each day for prayer, Bible reading, and quiet reflection. Perhaps you already do so. If you do, you might like to devote a short time each day to memorizing the Word of God, in addition to your other endeavors.

If you are completely new to all of this and don't spend any time alone in spiritual meditation, here are some suggestions.

Find a place that is quiet and completely private. Where there are no distractions, like a spouse, children, pets, TV, stereo, etc. Some people actually like quiet reflective music, void of lyrics, in the background. One of my rooms once had a fountain with the gentle sound of a waterfall continually providing a relaxing mood and atmosphere. It was wonderful until the pump broke. Then after I got used to complete quiet again, I never replaced the pump.

The important thing is that wherever you practice you are alone and undisturbed.

Find a comfortable chair or place to lay down in a correctly aligned posture that is conducive for an extended time in that position.

When you start off, set aside a short period of time, like 10 or 15 minutes to begin with. But commit to do that for one week. Don't miss a day. That will begin to establish a discipline in your practice. Then, take it from there on how you want to continue.

If early morning is not convenient, any time in the day will also be a good time to practice. Some people like to practice in the evening or just before bedtime. Just turn off the TV for 30 minutes each night and you will have plenty of time.

There is almost always time available to do the activities you really want to do. How you arrange your schedule is the true measurement of what your heart really desires.

Which Bible Translation
to Memorize

I n the beginning, there was only one version of the Bible to
memorize. And it was written in Hebrew. This was the
Torah, or the first five books (Genesis, Exodus, Leviticus,
Numbers, and Deuteronomy), that most Jewish and Christian
theologians have traditionally agreed was given directly by
God to Moses.

The Hebrew word *torah* literally means "teaching or
instruction". Therefore, in Jewish tradition, the first
five books of the Bible are considered "the teachings and
instructions of God". To this day it is generally part of the
liturgy in Jewish synagogues that the huge scroll the Torah
is written upon, before it is opened to be read from, is
ceremoniously carried about the sanctuary so that all may have
an opportunity to touch it with their hand, Bible, or the
tzit-tzit (tassel) of their prayer shawl, and then touch that
object to their lips as a sign of reverence and devotion. Later
they all stand, point toward the Torah, and in unison profess,

"This is the Torah that Moses placed before the children of Israel, at the command of the LORD, through Moses' hand." (Deut. 4:44 and Num. 9:23)

In Jewish tradition, the Torah is held in slightly greater significance than the other books of the Bible because of its method of transmission. It is believed that the Torah was given directly by God to Moses and then to the people. It is a unique combination of divine oracle and divine inspiration. All the other books of the Bible are believed to be inspired by God through the writer of that book. The fact of their inspiration had to be agreed upon at a later date by the religious leaders of their day. It is not always clear just how this agreement process took place in each case. This is not to dispute their divine authority, but merely to emphasize the unique quality of the Torah.

There are exactly 304,805 letters in a Torah scroll. If even one letter is found to be extra or missing, the entire scroll is considered invalid. Even the writing of each letter must conform to *Halakhic* (legal) rules according to rabbinic tradition. The Hebrew word for scribe is *sofer*. The word itself is related to the Hebrew word for counting. A qualified *Sofer* continually counts lines, the letters on each line, and even the spaces between words and letters. Every letter is considered precious. There is a saying attributed to one of the ancient Jewish sages that if even one letter is added or deleted from the Torah, it will destroy the world.

So you can begin to see that when someone commits to translating the Word of God into another language, great care must be taken. Just using any particular word and then claiming it to be the translated "Word of God" is highly questionable.

It's beyond the scope of this book to delve into the history of how the various books of the Bible eventually came to be gathered together and canonized. The point I do want to make is that the original language that both Jews and Christians believe God transmitted His word to us was in Hebrew.

The original group of books gathered together form the Hebrew Bible, commonly called the *Tanach* in Judaism or the Old Testament in Christianity. The word Tanach is an acronym for the letters – tet (T), nun (N), and chet (Ch) – which are the first letters in the Hebrew words – *Torah*, *Neviim*, and *Chetuvim* (*Torah*, Prophets and Writings). This is the order of the books in the Hebrew Bible.

Protestant Christianity uses these same books (Catholicism includes a few more) in a slightly different order based upon the Septuagint. This was one of the first translations of the original Hebrew into another language, *Koine* Greek, in about 250 B.C. Christians refer to this collection as the Old Testament to distinguish it apart from the New Testament, which was believed to be originally also written almost entirely in *Koine* Greek.

Actually both the Old Testament and the New Testament also have some brief passages or scattered words in Aramaic as well. But for the most part, these two languages – Hebrew for the *Tanach* or Old Testament and Greek for the New Testament – are the original languages of the Bible. Anything other than these languages is a translation!

With any translation there are always different ways of expressing essentially the same word, phrase or idea. It therefore becomes an opinion of the translator as to which way is the best. And with any opinion, there is always the possibility of personal bias or error creeping in.

With something as important as a book that professes itself to be the actual Word of God, this possibility of bias or error is extremely significant.

So it is with great consideration we must choose the right translation of the Bible if we are going to begin a process of committing large portions of it to our memory.

It's not enough to simply say, "Oh, this is what we use at my Church or Synagogue." Or, "This is what I've always used in the past."

Let me begin by stating a basic fact. There are **no** perfect translations! The original text is perfect. The translation is not. All translations are less than perfect derivatives of the original text. This is not only due to the human element of bias or error. But also the essential differences of various languages. Not every word in every language has a truly comparable word in another language.

For example, Proverbs 9:10 in most English translations reads something like:

The <u>fear</u> of the LORD is the beginning of wisdom:
and the knowledge of the holy is understanding.   *KJV*

The actual Hebrew word usually translated as "fear" is *yirah*. But according to the ancient Jewish sages this word had a dual meaning as there are two categories of *yirah*, depending upon the context. The lower form is the primal fear of harm or punishment. But the higher form is one of awe and reverence. In a way, they reflect the two emotions of fear and reverence that the Hebrew people must have felt when they all stood at the foot of Mount Horeb (Sinai) and first heard the voice of God speak to them in a national revelation. The understanding of these two different emotions combined into one cannot be fully explained with the single English word "fear".

In addition, every language uses idioms, which are words or phrases that have a cultural meaning apart from the literal meaning. Both Hebrew and Greek have idioms unique to them which when translated directly sometimes can be confusing.

For example, in Matthew 6:23 Jesus says,

But if thine eye be <u>evil</u>,
thy whole body shall be full of darkness.

Some translations use the word "bad" instead of "evil". The actual Greek word used here is *poneros* which does mean literally hurtful or evil. However the concept of someone having an "evil eye" in ancient times was not meant literally, but rather referred to someone who was greedy or selfish.

To try to deal with some of these difficulties, two main approaches to Biblical translations have developed.

One method is called the **formal equivalency** approach. This method is also referred to as the **word-for-word** approach. This was the earliest method used in translations such as the King James Version (KJV) and the New King James Version (NKJV). The early Jewish Publication Society (JPS) editions, which relied heavily on the KJV for its text, also used this approach.

This method tries to stay as close to the original text as possible by simply finding the best English word choice or choices for each original Hebrew or Greek word. Adjustments have to be made in sentence structure because of the differences in the grammatical rules of the languages. But when following this method, the resulting English translation also reveals an insight into the original language not only by the words, but how they are combined into phrases, clauses and sentences.

The greatest example of the formal equivalency method is undeniably the King James Version (KJV). It was originally published in 1611, then later revised in 1615, 1629, 1638 and finally in 1762. This single book has been hailed by literary scholars over the years not only as the most influential book of all time, but as the single greatest example of English literature ever published.

Originally 54 scholars, most of whom were fluent in Hebrew, Greek and numerous ancient languages, labored for over seven years to produce the masterpiece commissioned by King James I. They relied mainly on the Hebrew Masoretic text for the Old Testament, which had been used for centuries by the Jewish Rabbis as the only version of the Tanach. For the New Testament they relied mainly on the Textus Receptus, commonly known as the Received Text or the Byzantine Greek Text. In later years some debate has arisen concerning which texts of the New Testament are more reliable. Those discussions are beyond the scope of this book. For anyone interested in learning more on that I recommend the book *Which Version is the Bible* by Floyd Nolen Jones for an interesting exploration of that subject.

In recent years another direction in translation has emerged called the **dynamic equivalency** approach, also known as the **thought-for-thought** approach. The most popular example of this method is the *New International Version (NIV)*. Using this method, the translators give their opinion not only as to the best word choice, but also what they consider the original writer actually meant to say! One can immediately see an enormous problem arising here. To begin with, how can anyone really know what another writer actually meant to say? But to make matters worse, if that original writer is believed to actually be writing under the inspiration of God, then the translator is essentially claiming the ability to better explain the Bible than God could do Himself. This notion should give anyone who is honestly seeking the truth of the Holy Scriptures some pause.

Certainly thought-for-thought translations can be more easily read sometimes. But the potential for personal bias and error runs rampant in these translations.

Another problem arises with the thought-for-thought method. One of the primary rules of English composition is the principal of omitting unnecessary words. It is interesting that when you read the Bible in the original Hebrew or Greek texts you realize that there are **no** unnecessary words in them! Every word is essential and important. This perfection of composition brings a poetic quality to the original text that makes any translation difficult to match. The best way to try and reveal that perfection is by the word-for-word approach rather than thought-for-thought.

These are some of the reasons I've chosen mainly the King James Version (KJV) for my personal choice as the best Bible translation for memory work. However, each person has their own personal preferences. So you might prefer another translation and that's fine. Whichever translation you choose, the fundamental principles of memorization explained in this book will apply to your memory work.

But since I am recommending the KJV as a personal choice, in the next section I'm going to discuss some potential challenges with using the KJV and some suggestions on how to best address these.

Optimizing the Translation

Although we will mainly be dealing with some of the particular challenges associated with the KJV in this section, most of these principals can also be applied to any translation that you choose to use for your memory work.

The most common complaint I hear from people regarding the KJV is the archaic Elizabethan vernacular of the prose. Nobody talks that way anymore. Someone complained to me once, "All of those thee's and thou's makes it sound like Shakespeare!" In fact, 1611, the first year of its publication, was also the year that Shakespeare started work on his last play, The Tempest.

But before one simply dismisses the KJV on this point, perhaps I can suggest that we first make an attempt to better understand Elizabethan English and realize some of its actual advantages over our modern way of using the English language.

There is a theory that languages tend to evolve regressively over time and become more simplified with usage over generations. This certainly is the case with the English language. A perfect example is how modern English deals with the second-person singular and plural form.

Hebrew and Greek, as well as Elizabethan English, have different words or word endings to distinguish the second-person singular and plural form. Modern English only has one form to distinguish both. Let me explain:

In Matthew 5:14, for example, when Jesus says . . .

Ye are the light of the world.
A city that is set on an hill cannot he hid. *KJV*

This is usually translated into modern English something like . . .

You are the light of the world.
A city that is set on a hill cannot be hid.

We would not really know, except by the context of the previous and following verses whether Jesus was speaking to one person or many.

However, in the original Koine Greek text we know that Jesus is speaking to more than one person because the Greek word translated as **ye** is nominative plural.

Elizabethan English has different words to make that distinction. Modern English does not.

Here is the rule:

Second-person singular - thee, thou, thine.

Second-person plural - you, ye, yours.

The important thing to realize is that both Hebrew and Koine Greek do distinguish between second-person singular and plural. Therefore one cannot fully understand this aspect of either of these languages while reading them translated into modern English. Part of the simplification process of the English language over the years has been the combining of the second-person singular and plural into one indistinguishable form. This may make it easier for us as English speakers today. But it becomes critical in many Bible verses, particularly in many of the prophetic verses. After a little experience with the forms of second-person in the KJV, it actually becomes much more insightful when reading the scriptures.

Another characteristic of Elizabethan English are the "st" and "th" endings on verbs associated with second-person pronouns. These endings are no longer used today in modern English and seem almost foreign. But if you notice, they often add a musical and poetic quality to the language that is very distinct. Compare Psalm 23 or the Lord's Prayer in the KJV with any other translation. There is simply no comparison. These translations in the KJV are models of perfection. This is exactly how the Word of God truly is.

Here is another way of looking at it. When we read Elizabethan English today, although we understand it, the prose seems almost foreign at times. It's like reading a foreign language that we can understand, but doesn't exactly seem our native tongue. That's the way I like to look at Elizabethan English. It's like learning a foreign language that is very similar to our own native language, but just slightly different at times. When you become proficient at Elizabethan English it's like becoming multi-lingual in a way. And learning another language is always a worthwhile achievement. It actually increases your intelligence because it causes your brain to expand its ability to process and organize your thoughts.

In a way, it's the next best thing to reading the text in the original Hebrew or Greek, which is actually the best way to memorize the Bible. But that is a subject and process for another book and beyond the desire of most people. Besides, it really isn't necessary if you have a good translation.

Another suggestion I can make with regard to optimizing your translation involves some personal study on your own. Remember I stated earlier that no perfect translation exists because of the limitations of the translation problems of one language to another. It ultimately comes down to a matter of the personal opinion of every translator which word choices to use.

One of the ways that I personally deal with this area is that I become my own translator with regard to certain word choices that I feel will be an improvement of the original translation. Now I am not recommending just randomly changing the wording of the KJV here! But there are certain words that could be improved upon.

For example, whenever the word "law" appears in the Old Testament I invariably find that the actual Hebrew word used

is *torah*. As I stated earlier, *torah* actually means teachings
or instructions. As English speakers, when we think of "law"
we tend to think of the commandments. But the Hebrew
word for commandments is *mitzvot*. This is the plural form.
The singular form would be *mitzvah*. This word mitzvah has
actually entered into our English language and can also be
defined as an act fulfilling a commandment, such as doing an
act of charity.

As I stated earlier, the Torah, in Jewish tradition refers to
the first five books of the Bible. But in the broader sense, the
word *torah*, when used in the context as the teachings and
instructions of God, can also apply to the entire Bible. The
entire Bible is the teachings and instructions of God. So
therefore, the entire Bible, all of the Word of God is *torah*!

So when I recite any verse from the Old Testament that
uses the word "law", I use the word *torah* instead. What could
be a better word choice than that? I am using the original
Hebrew word! In fact I substitute many of the original
Hebrew words from the Old Testament when I memorize
my personal collection of Bible verses. Because I've studied
Hebrew and I enjoy practicing my Hebrew and interposing it
in key passages of the Bible where the true meaning of a word
is best revealed by simply using the original word.

Now this may not be for everybody. But it adds a personal
touch to my own Bible memory work that I find invaluable.
It also encourages me to do some independent Bible study
from the original text in both the Hebrew and Greek as to
just what actually was written. I've found that every Bible
translation, including the KJV, has a doctrinal bias. Christian

translations have a Christian bias and Jewish translations have a Jewish bias. The KJV has a definite Protestant Christian bias. At times, it even seems to have an anti-Jewish bias in some of its word choices, which reflects an unfortunate anti-Semitism that was rampant in the Christian world then and to some extent still exists today.

This is not a reason to reject the KJV. But rather simply to make an occasional modification in some of its word choices that provides the most accurate translation possible. This can also be applied to some of the archaic words, such as "froward", which are almost never used today. In the selected verses I've included later in the Memory Book, you will see examples of these modifications.

The Nature of Hebrew Poetry

All languages consist of primarily two elements – words and grammar. Words are like the flesh that we see and grammar the hidden skeleton that holds it all together. Words are the individual sounds that have meaning while grammar represents the ways that we organize our thoughts. There are a multitude of sounds in every language and each has its own unique meaning. But there are certain fundamental principles in the way we all organize our thinking and this brings a similarity to how all languages are constructed. We all have similar ways of organizing our thinking because we are all created in the image of the same God.

Etymology, which is the study of word origins, has shown how word sounds often carry over from one language to another when languages intermingle. This is also true to some degree with grammatical structure. The ways that people organize their thinking will greatly affect their written literature, as well.

As Christians and Jews, we believe that the Holy Bible is the inspired Word of God. We may have disagreements as to exactly which books make up the Bible. We may also disagree in the interpretation of the Bible and different doctrines of faith that reflect these differences. But if we simply look at those books that all Christians and Jews can agree upon as being inspired of God, we can draw some interesting observations. One of these observations is that God is the greatest author of all time! There has never been a single human author who can match the great literary excellence found in the Bible. The Bible has formed the basis for all resulting written literature, codes of law, measure of poetic quality and historic record. Even the very fact that all people in the world measure time in terms of a seven day week comes from the Bible. The entire world now records history relative to the birth before or after Jesus. If you want to determine which of all the religions in the world the one true religion is, simply compare the books they claim as inspired of God. The Holy Bible will always win over all others.

The purpose of this book is not commentary on the Bible. But to help in your memory work, it is useful to understand something about the poetic structure that so much of it is written in. God is the greatest poet of all time and His Word reflects that fact.

In this chapter we are going to look more closely at the structure of Hebrew poetry as it relates to the Bible. The poetical books are generally considered to be – Job, Psalms, Proverbs, Ecclesiastes, and the Song of Solomon (Song of

Songs). However, much of the writings of the Prophets are written in the poetical style, as well. The Book of Isaiah, for example, is filled with the beautiful poetic verse structure that we find in the Psalms.

A common characteristic of English poetry rhymes the last words in lines. Hebrew poetry rhymes ideas, rather than words. This principle is known as **parallelism**. There are at least six types of parallelism found in the Old Testament.

Synonymous - Two consecutive lines are similar in meaning, in that they express the same or similar idea, but in a slightly different way.

Yea, it thou criest after knowledge,
and liftest up thy voice for understanding;

Prov. 2:3

Thy word is a lamp unto my feet,
and a light unto my path.

Psalm 119:105

Antithetic - The second line contrasts with the first.

The wicked are overthrown, and are not:
but the house of the righteous shall stand.

Prov. 12:7

The heart of the wise is in the house of mourning;
but the heart of fools is in the house of mirth.

Eccles. 7:4

Synthetic - The second line further develops the idea of the first line.

For the LORD is a great God,
and a great King above all gods.

Psalm 95:3

The LORD reigneth; let the earth rejoice;
let the multitude of isles be glad thereof.

Psalm 97:1

Emblematic - One line declares the main point while another line or lines illustrates it with an image or example.

Harden not your heart, as in the provocation,
and as in the day of temptation in the wilderness:
When your fathers tempted me,
proved me, and saw my work.

Psalm 95:8-9

As the hart panteth after the water brooks,
so panteth my soul after thee, O God.

Psalm 42:1

Climactic - The second line repeats the first line but changes the ending.

Thou art my God, and I will praise thee:
thou art my God, I will exalt thee.

Psalm 118:28

O sing unto the LORD a new song:
sing unto the LORD, all the earth.

Psalm 96:1

Formal -   Two or more lines are joined together without any of the above relationships.

I laid me down and slept; I awaked;
for the LORD sustained me.

Psalm 3:5

Make me to go in the path of thy commandments;
for therein do I delight.

Psalm 119:35

This is a brief introduction into some basic elements of Hebrew poetry found in the Bible. It is helpful knowledge in conjunction with your memory work. But all serious students of the Bible should continue with study of commentary from a variety of Christian, Messianic and traditional Jewish sources.

9

Memory Book

n this section we present an extensive collection of verses as an example of a **Memory Book** laid out in the **E-Z Memory Format**. Hopefully we have included some that comprise popular favorites. The hardest part was leaving out others simply due to lack of space. Those you can include later in your own personal Memory Book.

Words that are followed by (*) show how you can modify the original text to clarify certain words.

I hope that what you have read so far has been helpful. And my prayer is that as you memorize the Word of God it will be a blessing to you for many years to come.

Psalms

Psalm 1

B lessed is the man that walketh not
in the counsel of the ungodly,
nor standeth in the way of sinners,
nor sitteth in the seat of the scornful.

But his delight is in the law* of the LORD;   *(torah)
and in his law doth he meditate day and night.

And he shall be like a tree
planted by the rivers of water,
that bringeth forth his fruit in his season;
his leaf also shall not wither;
and whatsoever he doeth shall prosper.

The ungodly are not so:
but are like the chaff which the wind driveth away.

Therefore the ungodly shall not stand in the judgment,
nor sinners in the congregation of the righteous.

For the LORD knoweth the way of the righteous:
but the way of the ungodly shall perish.

Psalm 19

The heavens declare the glory of God;
and the firmament sheweth* his handiwork. *(showeth)

Day unto day uttereth speech,
and night unto night sheweth knowledge.

There is no speech nor language,
where their voice is not heard.

Their line is gone out through all of the earth,
and their words to the end of the world.
In them hath he set a tabernacle for the sun,

Which is as a bridegroom coming out of his chamber,
and rejoiceth as a strong man to run a race.

His going forth is from the end of the heaven,
and his circuit unto the ends of it:
and there is nothing hid from the heat thereof.

The law of the LORD is perfect, converting the soul:
the testimony of the LORD is sure, making wise the simple.

The statutes of the LORD are right, rejoicing the heart:
the commandment of the LORD is pure, enlightening the eyes.

The fear of the LORD is clean, enduring for ever:
the judgments of the LORD are true and righteous altogether.

More to be desired are they than gold,
yea, than much fine gold:
sweeter also than honey and the honeycomb.

Moreover by them is thy servant warned:
and in keeping of them there is great reward.

Who can understand his errors?
cleanse thou me from secret faults.

Keep back thy servant also from presumptuous sins;
let them not have dominion over me:
then shall I be upright,
and I shall be innocent from the great transgression.

Let the words of my mouth,
and the meditation of my heart,
be acceptable in thy sight, O LORD,
my strength, and my redeemer.

Psalm 23

The LORD is my shepherd; I shall not want.

He maketh me to lie down in green pastures:
he leadeth me beside the still waters.

He restoreth my soul:
he leadeth me in the paths of righteousness
for his name's sake.

Yea, though I walk
through the valley of the shadow of death,
I will fear no evil: for thou art with me;
thy rod and thy staff they comfort me.

Thou preparest a table before me
in the presence of mine enemies:
thou anointest my head with oil;
my cup runneth over.

Surely goodness and mercy
shall follow me all the days of my life:
and I will dwell in the house of the LORD for ever.

Psalm 91

He that dwelleth in the secret place of the most High
shall abide under the shadow of the Almighty.

I will say of the LORD,
He is my refuge and my fortress:
my God; in him will I trust.

Surely he shall deliver thee
from the snare of the fowler,
and from the noisome pestilence.

He shall cover thee with his feathers,
and under his wings shalt thou trust:
his truth shall be thy shield and buckler.

Thou shalt not be afraid for the terror by night;
nor for the arrow that flieth by day;

Nor for the pestilence that walketh in darkness;
nor for the destruction that wasteth at noonday.

A thousand shall fall at thy side,
and ten thousand at thy right hand;
but it shall not come nigh thee.

Only with thine eyes shalt thou behold and see
the reward of the wicked.

Because thou hast made the LORD,
which is my refuge,
even the most High, thy habitation;

There shall no evil befall thee,
neither shall any plague come nigh thy dwelling.

For he shall give his angels charge over thee,
to keep thee in all thy ways.

They shall bear thee up in their hands,
lest thou dash thy foot against a stone.

Thou shalt tread upon the lion and adder:
the young lion and the dragon
shalt thou trample under feet.

Because he hath set his love upon me,
therefore will I deliver him:
I will set him on high, because he hath known my name.

He shall call upon me, and I will answer him:
I will be with him in trouble;
I will deliver him, and honour him.

With long life will I satisfy him,
and shew him my salvation.

Psalm 103

Bless the LORD, O my soul:
and all that is within me, bless his holy name.

Bless the LORD, O my soul,
and forget not all his benefits:

Who forgiveth all thine iniquities;
who healeth all thy diseases;

Who redeemeth thy life from destruction;
who crowneth thee with lovingkindness and tender mercies;

Who satisfieth thy mouth with good things;
so that thy youth is renewed like the eagle's.

The LORD executeth righteousness and judgment
for all that are oppressed.

He made known his ways unto Moses,
his acts unto the children of Israel.

The LORD is merciful and gracious,
slow to anger, and plenteous in mercy.

He will not always chide:
neither will he keep his anger for ever.

He hath not dealt with us after our sins;
nor rewarded us according to our iniquities.

For as the heaven is high above the earth,
so great is his mercy toward them that fear him.

As far as the east is from the west,
so far hath he removed our transgressions from us.

Like as a father pitieth his children,
so the LORD pitieth them that fear him.

For he knoweth our frame;
he remembereth that we are dust.

As for man, his days are as grass:
as a flower of the field, so he flourisheth.

For the wind passeth over it, and it is gone;
and the place thereof shall know it no more.

But the mercy of the LORD is from everlasting to everlasting
upon them that fear him,
and his righteousness unto children's children;

To such as keep his covenant,
and to those that remember his commandments
to do them.

The LORD hath prepared his throne in the heavens;
and his kingdom ruleth over all.

Bless the LORD, ye his angels,
that excel in strength, that do his commandments,
hearkening unto the voice of his word.

Bless ye the LORD, all ye his hosts;
ye ministers of his, that do his pleasure.

Bless the LORD, all his works in all places of his dominion:
bless the LORD, O my soul.

Psalm 119

ℵ Aleph

Blessed are the undefiled in the way,
who walk in the law of the LORD.

Blessed are they that keep his testimonies,
and that seek him with the whole heart.

They also do no iniquity: they walk in his ways.

Thou hast commanded us to keep thy precepts diligently.

O that my ways were directed to keep thy statutes!

Then shall I not be ashamed,
when I have respect unto all thy commandments.

I will praise thee with uprightness of heart,
when I shall have learned thy righteous judgments.

I will keep thy statutes: O forsake me not utterly.

ב Bet

Wherewithal shall a young man cleanse his way?
by taking heed thereto according to thy word.

With my whole heart have I sought thee:
O let me not wander from thy commandments.

Thy word have I hid in mine heart,
that I might not sin against thee.

Blessed art thou, O LORD: teach me thy statutes.

With my lips have I declared
all the judgments of thy mouth.

I have rejoiced in the way of thy testimonies,
as much as in all riches.

I will meditate in thy precepts,
and have respect unto thy ways.

I will delight myself in thy statutes:
I will not forget thy word.

Psalm 121

I will lift up mine eyes unto the hills,
from whence cometh my help.

My help cometh from the LORD,
which made heaven and earth.

He will not suffer thy foot to be moved:
he that keepeth thee will not slumber.

Behold, he that keepeth Israel
shall neither slumber nor sleep.

The LORD is thy keeper:
the LORD is thy shade upon thy right hand.

The sun shall not smite thee by day, nor the moon by night.

The LORD shall preserve thee from all evil:
he shall preserve thy soul.

The LORD shall preserve thy going out and thy coming in
from this time forth, and even for evermore.

Psalm 139

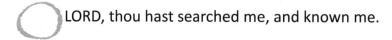LORD, thou hast searched me, and known me.

Thou knowest my downsitting and mine uprising,
thou understandest my thought afar off.

Thou compassest my path and my lying down,
and art acquainted with all my ways.

For there is not a word in my tongue,
but, lo, O LORD, thou knowest it altogether.

Thou has beset me behind and before,
and laid thine hand upon me.

Such knowledge is too wonderful for me;
it is high, I cannot attain unto it.

Whither shall I go from thy spirit?
or whither shall I flee from thy presence?

If I ascend up into heaven, thou art there:
if I make my bed in hell, behold, thou art there.

If I take the wings of the morning,
and dwell in the uttermost parts of the sea;

Even there shall thy hand lead me,
and thy right hand shall hold me.

If I say, Surely the darkness shall cover me;
even the night shall be light about me.

Yea, the darkness hideth not from thee;
but the night shineth as the day:
the darkness and the light are both alike to thee.

For thou hast possessed my reins:
thou has covered me in my mother's womb.

I will praise thee;
for I am fearfully and wonderfully made:
marvellous are thy works;
and that my soul knoweth right well.

My substance was not hid from thee,
when I was made in secret,
and curiously wrought in the lowest parts of the earth.

Thine eyes did see my substance, yet being unperfect;
and in thy book all my members were written,
which in continuance were fashioned,
when as yet there was none of them.

How precious also are thy thoughts unto me, O God!
how great is the sum of them!

If I should count them,
they are more in number than the sand:
when I awake, I am still with thee.

Surely thou wilt slay the wicked, O God:
depart from me therefore, ye bloody men.

For they speak against thee wickedly,
and thine enemies take thy name in vain.

Do not I hate* them, O LORD, that hate thee?   *(reject)
and am not I grieved with those that rise up against thee?

I hate them with perfect hatred:
I count them mine enemies.

Search me, O God, and know my heart:
try me, and know my thoughts:

And see if there be any wicked way in me,
and lead me in the way everlasting.

Proverbs

Proverbs 3

My son, forget not my law;
but let thine heart keep my commandments;

For length of days, and long life, and peace,
shall they add to thee.

Let not mercy and truth forsake thee:
bind them about thy neck;
write them upon the table of thine heart:

So shalt thou find favour and good understanding
in the sight of God and man.

Trust in the LORD with all thine heart;
and lean not unto thine own understanding.

In all thy ways acknowledge him, and he shall direct thy paths.

Be not wise in thine own eyes:
fear the LORD, and depart from evil.

It shall be health to thy navel, and marrow to thy bones.

Honour the LORD with thy substance,
and with the firstfruits of all thine increase:

So shall thy barns be filled with plenty,
and thy presses shall burst out with new wine.

My son, despise not the chastening of the LORD;
neither be weary of his correction:

For whom the LORD loveth he correcteth;
even as a father the son in whom he delighteth.

Happy is the man that findeth wisdom,
and the man that getteth understanding.

For the merchandise of it is better
than the merchandise of silver,
and the gain thereof than fine gold.

She is more precious than rubies:
and all the things thou canst desire
are not to be compared unto her.

Length of days is in her right hand;
and in her left hand riches and honour.

Her ways are ways of pleasantness,
and all her paths are peace.

She is a tree of life to them that lay hold upon her:
and happy is every one that retaineth her.

The LORD by wisdom hath founded the earth;
by understanding hath he established the heavens.

By his knowledge the depths are broken up,
and the clouds drop down the dew.

My son, let not them depart from thine eyes:
keep sound wisdom and discretion:

So shall they be life unto thy soul,
and grace to thy neck.

Then shalt thou walk in thy way safely,
and thy foot shall not stumble.

When thou liest down, thou shalt not be afraid:
yea, thou shalt lie down, and thy sleep shall be sweet.

Be not afraid of sudden fear,
neither of the desolation of the wicked, when it cometh.

For the LORD shall be thy confidence,
and shall keep thy foot from being taken.

Withhold not good from them to whom it is due,
when it is in the power of thine hand to do it.

Say not unto thy neighbour, Go, and come again,
and tomorrow I will give; when thou hast it by thee.

Devise not evil against thy neighbour,
seeing he dwelleth securely by thee.

Strive not with a man without cause,
if he have done thee no harm.

Envy thou not the oppressor, and choose none of his ways.

For the froward* is abomination to the LORD: *(perverse)
but his secret is with the righteous.

The curse of the LORD is in the house of the wicked:
but he blesseth the habitation of the just.

Surely he scorneth the scorners:
but he giveth grace unto the lowly.

The wise shall inherit glory:
but shame shall be the promotion of fools.

Proverbs 6:16-23

These six things doth the LORD hate:
yea, seven are an abomination unto him:

A proud look, a lying tongue,
and hands that shed innocent blood,

An heart that deviseth wicked imaginations,
feet that be swift in running to mischief*,   *(evil)

A false witness that speaketh lies,
and he that soweth discord among brethren.

My son, keep thy father's commandment,
and forsake not the law of thy mother:

Bind them continually upon thine heart,
and tie them about thy neck.

When thou goest, it shall lead thee;
when thou sleepest, it shall keep thee;
and when thou awakest, it shall talk with thee.

For the commandment is a lamp; and the law is light;
and reproofs of instruction are the way of life:

Proverbs 28:9

He that turneth away his ear from hearing the law,
even his prayer shall be abomination.

Proverbs 28:26

He that trusteth in his own heart is a fool:
but whoso walketh wisely, he shall be delivered.

Exodus

Exodus 3:1-8

Now Moses kept the flock of Jethro
his father in law, the priest of Midian:
and he led the flock to the backside of the desert,
and came to the mountain of God,
even to Horeb.

And the angel of the LORD appeared unto him
in a flame of fire out of the midst of a bush:
and he looked, and, behold,
the bush burned with fire,
and the bush was not consumed.

And Moses said,
I will now turn aside, and see this great sight,
why the bush is not burnt.

And when the LORD saw that he turned aside to see,
God called unto him out of the midst of the bush,
and said, Moses, Moses.
And he said, Here am I.

And he said, Draw not nigh hither:
put off thy shoes from off thy feet,
for the place whereon thou standest is holy ground.

Moreover he said,
I am the God of thy father,
the God of Abraham, the God of Isaac, and the God of Jacob.
And Moses hid his face;
for he was afraid to look upon God.

And the LORD said,
I have surely seen the affliction of my people
which are in Egypt,
and have heard their cry by reason of their taskmasters;
for I know their sorrows;

And I am come down to deliver them
out of the hand of the Egyptians,
and to bring them up out of that land
unto a good land and a large,
unto a land flowing with milk and honey . . .

Exodus 3:13-15

And Moses said unto God,
      Behold, when I come unto the children of Israel,
and shall say unto them,
The God of your fathers hath sent me unto you;
and they shall say to me, What is his name?
what shall I say unto them?

And God said unto Moses,
I AM THAT I AM:
and he said,
Thus shalt thou say unto the children of Israel,
I AM hath sent me unto you.

And God said moreover unto Moses,
Thus shalt thou say unto the children of Israel,
The LORD God of your fathers,
the God of Abraham, the God of Isaac, and the God of Jacob,
hath sent me unto you:
this is my name for ever,
and this is my memorial unto all generations.

Exodus 19:3-11

And Moses went up unto God,
and the LORD called unto him out of the mountain, saying,
Thus shalt thou say to the house of Jacob,
and tell the children of Israel;

Ye have seen what I did unto the Egyptians,
and how I bare you on eagles' wings,
and brought you unto myself.

Now therefore, if ye will obey my voice indeed,
and keep my covenant,
then ye shall be a peculiar* treasure unto me
above all people: for all the earth is mine:

And ye shall be unto me a kingdom of priests,
and an holy nation.
These are the words which thou shalt speak
unto the children of Israel.

And Moses came
and called for the elders of the people,
and laid before their faces all these words
which the LORD commanded him.

And all the people answered together, and said,
All that the LORD hath spoken we will do.
And Moses returned the words of the people
unto the LORD.

And the LORD said unto Moses,
Lo, I come unto thee in a thick cloud,
that the people may hear when I speak with thee,
and believe thee for ever.
And Moses told the words of the people unto the LORD.

And the LORD said unto Moses,
Go unto the people,
and sanctify them to-day and tomorrow,
and let them wash their clothes,

And be ready against the third day:
for the third day the LORD will come down
in the sight of all the people upon mount Sinai.

peculiar* - This adjective does not appear in the Hebrew text. In the Torah the
single word is *segulah*, which is usually translated as "special or treasure". To call
someone a "peculiar treasure" has a negative connotation, rather than a positive one.
So in repeating this line, I choose to omit this word.

Exodus 19:16-21

And it came to pass on the third day in the morning,
that there were thunders and lightnings,
and a thick cloud upon the mount,
and the voice of the trumpet exceeding loud;
so that all the people that was in the camp trembled.

And Moses brought forth the people out of the camp
to meet with God;
and they stood at the nether part of the mount.

And mount Sinai was altogether on a smoke,
because the LORD descended upon it in fire:
and the smoke thereof ascended as the smoke of a furnace,
and the whole mount quaked greatly.

And when the voice of the trumpet sounded long,
and waxed louder and louder,
Moses spake, and God answered him by a voice.

And the LORD came down upon mount Sinai,
on the top of the mount:
and the LORD called Moses up to the top of the mount;
and Moses went up.

And the LORD said unto Moses,
Go down, charge the people,
lest they break through unto the LORD to gaze,
and many of them perish.

Exodus 20:1-22

A nd God spake all these words, saying,

I am the LORD thy God,
which have brought thee out of the land of Egypt,
out of the house of bondage.

Thou shalt have no other gods before me.

Thou shalt not make unto thee any graven image,
or any likeness of any thing that is in heaven above,
or that is in the earth beneath,
or that is in the water under the earth:

Thou shalt not bow down thyself to them, nor serve them:
For I the LORD thy God am a jealous God,
visiting the iniquity of the fathers upon the children
unto the third and fourth generation of them that hate me;

And shewing mercy unto thousands of them that love me,
and keep my commandments.

Thou shalt not take the name of the LORD thy God in vain;
for the LORD will not hold him guiltless
that taketh his name in vain.

Remember the sabbath day, to keep it holy.

Six days shalt thou labour, and do all thy work:

But the seventh day is the sabbath of the LORD thy God:
in it thou shalt not do any work,
thou, nor thy son, nor thy daughter,
thy manservant, nor thy maidservant,
nor thy cattle, nor the stranger that is within thy gates:

For in six days the LORD made heaven and earth,
the sea, and all that in them is,
and rested the seventh day:
wherefore the LORD blessed the sabbath day,
and hallowed it.

Honour thy father and thy mother:
that thy days may be long upon the land
which the LORD thy God giveth thee.

Thou shalt not kill*. *(murder)

Thou shalt not commit adultery.

Thou shalt not steal.

Thou shalt not bear false witness against thy neighbour.

Thou shalt not covet thy neighbour's house,
thou shalt not covet thy neighbour's wife,
nor his manservant, nor his maidservant,
nor his ox, nor his ass,
nor any thing that is thy neighbour's.

And all the people saw the thunderings, and the lightnings,
and the noise of the trumpet, and the mountain smoking:
and when the people saw it, they removed,
and stood afar off.

And they said unto Moses,
Speak thou with us, and we will hear:
but let not God speak with us, lest we die.

And Moses said unto the people,
Fear not: for God is come to prove you,
and that his fear may be before your faces,
that ye sin not.

And the people stood afar off,
and Moses drew near
unto the thick darkness where God was.

And the LORD said unto Moses,
Thus thou shalt say unto the children of Israel,
Ye have seen that I have talked with you from heaven.

Exodus 24:7-8

And he took the book of the covenant,
and read in the audience of the people:
and they said,
All that the LORD hath said will we do, and be obedient.

And Moses took the blood, and sprinkled it on the people,
and said, Behold the blood of the covenant
which the LORD hath made with you
concerning all these words.

Leviticus

Leviticus 17:11

For the life of the flesh is in the blood:
    and I have given it to you upon the altar
to make an atonement for your souls:
for it is the blood that maketh an atonement for the soul.

Leviticus 19:17-18

Thou shalt not hate thy brother in thine heart:
    thou shalt in any wise rebuke thy neighbour,
and not suffer sin upon him.

Thou shalt not avenge,
nor bear any grudge against the children of thy people,
but thou shalt love thy neighbour as thyself:
I am the LORD.

Leviticus 25:55

For unto me the children of Israel are servants;
they are my servants whom I brought forth
out of the land of Egypt: I am the LORD your God.

Leviticus 26:3-13

If ye walk in my statutes, and keep my commandments,
and do them;

Then I will give you rain in due season,
and the land shall yield her increase,
and the trees of the field shall yield their fruit.

And your threshing shall reach unto the vintage,
and the vintage shall reach unto the sowing time:
and ye shall eat your bread to the full,
and dwell in your land safely.

And I will give you peace in the land,
and ye shall lie down, and none shall make you afraid:
and I will rid evil beasts out of the land,
neither shall the sword go through your land.

And ye shall chase your enemies,
and they shall fall before you by the sword.

And five of you shall chase an hundred,

and an hundred of you shall put ten thousand to flight:

and your enemies shall fall before you by the sword.

For I will have respect unto you,

and make you fruitful, and multiply you,

and establish my covenant with you.

And ye shall eat old store,

and bring forth the old because of the new.

And I will set my tabernacle among you:

and my soul shall not abhor you.

And I will walk among you, and will be your God,

and ye shall be my people.

I am the LORD your God,

which brought you forth out of the land of Egypt,

that ye should not be their bondmen;

and I have broken the bands of your yoke,

and made you go upright.

Numbers

Numbers 15:37-41

And the LORD spake unto Moses, saying,

Speak unto the children of Israel,
and bid them that they make them fringes
in the borders of their garments
throughout their generations,
and that they put upon the fringe of the borders
a ribband of blue:

And it shall be unto you for a fringe,
that ye may look upon it,
and remember all the commandments of the LORD,
and do them; and that ye seek not
after your own heart and your own eyes,
after which ye use to go a-whoring:

That ye may remember, and do all my commandments,
and be holy unto your God.

I am the LORD your God,
which brought you out of the land of Egypt,
to be your God: I am the LORD your God.

Deuteronomy

Deut. 4:1-2

Now therefore hearken, O Israel,
unto the statutes and unto the judgments,
which I teach you, for to do them, that ye may live,
and go in and possess the land
which the LORD God of your fathers giveth you.

Ye shall not add unto the word which I command you,
neither shall ye diminish aught from it,
that ye may keep the commandments
of the LORD your God which I command you.

Deut. 4:5-9

Behold, I have taught you statutes and judgments,
even as the LORD my God commanded me,
that ye should do so in the land
whither ye go to possess it.

Keep therefore and do them;
for this is your wisdom and your understanding
in the sight of the nations,
which shall hear all these statutes, and say,
Surely this great nation is a wise and understanding people.

For what nation is there so great,
who hath God so nigh unto them,
as the LORD our God is in all things that we call upon him for?

And what nation is there so great,
that hath statutes and judgments so righteous as all this law,
which I set before you this day?

Only take heed to thyself, and keep thy soul diligently,
lest thou forget the things which thine eyes have seen,
and lest they depart from thy heart all the days of thy life:
but teach them thy sons, and thy sons' sons;

Deut. 6:4-9

Hear, O Israel: the LORD our God is one LORD:

And thou shalt love the LORD thy God with all thine heart,
and with all thy soul, and with all thy might.

And these words, which I command thee this day,
shall be in thine heart:

And thou shalt teach them diligently unto thy children,
and shalt talk of them when thou sittest in thine house,
and when thou walkest by the way,
and when thou liest down, and when thou risest up.

And thou shalt bind them for a sign upon thine hand,
and they shall be as frontlets between thine eyes.

And thou shalt write them upon the posts of thy house,
and on thy gates.

Deut. 7:6-15

For thou art an holy people unto the LORD thy God:
the LORD thy God hath chosen thee
to be a special people unto himself,
above all people that are upon the face of the earth.

The LORD did not set his love upon you, nor choose you,
because ye were more in number than any people;
for ye were the fewest of all people:

But because the LORD loved you,
and because he would keep the oath
which he had sworn unto your fathers,
hath the LORD brought you out with a mighty hand,
and redeemed you out of the house of bondmen,
from the hand of Pharaoh king of Egypt.

Know therefore that the LORD thy God,
he is God, the faithful God,
which keepeth covenant and mercy
with them that love him and keep his commandments
to a thousand generations;

And repayeth them that hate him to their face,
to destroy them:
he will not be slack to him that hateth him,
he will repay him to his face.

Thou shalt therefore keep the commandments,
and the statutes, and the judgments,
which I command thee this day, to do them.

Wherefore it shall come to pass,
if ye hearken to these judgments, and keep, and do them,
that the LORD thy God shall keep unto thee the covenant
and the mercy which he sware unto thy fathers:

And he will love thee, and bless thee, and multiply thee:
he will also bless the fruit of thy womb,
and the fruit of thy land,
thy corn, and thy wine, and thine oil,
the increase of thy kine, and the flocks of thy sheep,
in the land which he sware unto thy fathers to give thee.

Thou shalt be blessed above all people:
there shall not be male or female barren among you,
or among your cattle.

And the LORD will take away from thee all sickness,
and will put none of the evil diseases of Egypt,
which thou knowest, upon thee;
but will lay them upon all them that hate thee.

Deut. 10:12-19

And now, Israel,
what doth the LORD thy God require of thee,
but to fear the LORD thy God, to walk in all his ways,
and to love him,
and to serve the LORD thy God
with all thy heart and with all thy soul,

To keep the commandments of the LORD, and his statutes,
which I command thee this day for thy good?

Behold, the heaven and the heaven of heavens
is the LORD'S thy God,
the earth also, with all that therein is.

Only the LORD had a delight in thy fathers to love them,
and he chose their seed after them,
even you above all people, as it is this day.

Circumcise therefore the foreskin of your heart,
and be no more stiffnecked.

For the LORD your God is God of gods, and Lord of lords,
a great God, a mighty, and a terrible,
which regardeth not persons, nor taketh reward:

He doth execute the judgment of the fatherless and widow,
and loveth the stranger, in giving him food and raiment.

Love ye therefore the stranger:
for ye were strangers in the land of Egypt.

Deut. 29:29

The secret things belong unto the LORD our God:
but those things which are revealed
belong unto us and to our children for ever,
that we may do all the words of this law.

Deut. 30:11-20

For this commandment which I command thee this day,
it is not hidden from thee, neither is it far off.

It is not in heaven, that thou shouldest say,
Who shall go up for us to heaven, and bring it unto us,
that we may hear it, and do it?

Neither is it beyond the sea, that thou shouldest say,
Who shall go over the sea for us, and bring it unto us,
that we may hear it, and do it?

But the word is very nigh unto thee,
in thy mouth, and in thy heart,
that thou mayest do it.

See, I have set before thee this day life and good,
and death and evil;

In that I command thee this day to love the LORD thy God,
to walk in his ways, and to keep his commandments
and his statutes and his judgments,
that thou mayest live and multiply:
and the LORD thy God shall bless thee in the land
whither thou goest to possess it.

But if thine heart turn away, so that thou wilt not hear,
but shalt be drawn away,
and worship other gods, and serve them;

I denounce unto you this day, that ye shall surely perish,
and that ye shall not prolong your days upon the land,
whither thou passest over Jordan to go to possess it.

I call heaven and earth to record this day against you,
that I have set before you life and death,
blessing and cursing:
therefore choose life,
that both thou and thy seed may live:

That thou mayest love the LORD thy God,
and that thou mayest obey his voice,
and that thou mayest cleave unto him:
for he is thy life, and the length of thy days:
that thou mayest dwell in the land
which the LORD sware unto thy fathers,
to Abraham, to Isaac, and to Jacob, to give them.

Joshua

Joshua 1:8-9

This book of the law shall not depart out of thy mouth;
but thou shalt meditate therein day and night,
that thou mayest observe to do
according to all that is written therein:
for then thou shalt make thy way prosperous,
and then thou shalt have good success.

Have not I commanded thee? Be strong and of a good courage;
be not afraid, neither be thou dismayed:
for the LORD thy God is with thee whithersoever thou goest.

Ruth

Ruth 1:16

And Ruth said,
Entreat me not to leave thee,
or to return from following after thee:
for whither thou goest, I will go;
and where thou lodgest, I will lodge:
thy people shall be my people, and thy God my God:

1 Samuel

1 Samuel 2:1-10

And Hannah prayed, and said,
My heart rejoiceth in the LORD,
mine horn is exalted in the LORD:
my mouth is enlarged over mine enemies;
because I rejoice in thy salvation.

There is none holy as the LORD:
for there is none beside thee:
neither is there any rock like our God.

Talk no more so exceeding proudly;
let not arrogancy come out of your mouth:
for the LORD is a God of knowledge,
and by him actions are weighed.

The bows of the mighty men are broken,
and they that stumbled are girded with strength.

They that were full have hired out themselves for bread;
and they that were hungry ceased:
so that the barren hath born seven;
and she that hath many children is waxed feeble.

The LORD killeth, and maketh alive:
he bringeth down to the grave, and bringeth up.

The LORD maketh poor, and maketh rich:
he bringeth low, and lifteth up.

He raiseth up the poor out of the dust,
and lifteth up the beggar from the dunghill,
to set them among princes,
and to make them inherit the throne of glory:
for the pillars of the earth are the LORD'S,
and he hath set the world upon them.

He will keep the feet of his saints,
and the wicked shall be silent in darkness;
for by strength shall no man prevail.

The adversaries of the LORD shall be broken to pieces;
out of heaven shall he thunder upon them:
the LORD shall judge the ends of the earth;
and he shall give strength unto his king,
and exalt the horn of his anointed.

1 Samuel 15:22-23

And Samuel said, Hath the LORD as great delight
in burnt offerings and sacrifices,
as in obeying the voice of the LORD?
Behold, to obey is better than sacrifice,
and to hearken than the fat of rams.

For rebellion is as the sin of witchcraft,
and stubbornness is as iniquity and idolatry.
Because thou hast rejected the word of the LORD,
he hath also rejected thee from being king.

1 Samuel 16:7

But the LORD said unto Samuel,
Look not on his countenance,
or on the height of his stature;
because I have refused him:
for the LORD seeth not as man seeth;

for man looketh on the outward appearance,
but the LORD looketh on the heart.

1 Samuel 17:45-47

Then said David to the Philistine,
   Thou comest to me with a sword, and with a spear,
and with a shield:
but I come to thee in the name of the LORD of hosts,
the God of the armies of Israel, whom thou hast defied.

This day will the LORD deliver thee into mine hand;
and I will smite thee, and take thine head from thee;
and I will give the carcases
of the host of the Philistines this day
unto the fowls of the air, and to the wild beasts of the earth;
that all the earth may know that there is a God in Israel.

And all this assembly shall know
that the LORD saveth not with sword and spear:
for the battle is the LORD'S,
and he will give you into our hands.

Ecclesiastes

Eccles. 3

To every thing there is a season,
and a time to every purpose under the heaven:

A time to be born, and a time to die;
a time to plant, and a time to pluck up that which is planted;

A time to kill, and a time to heal;
a time to break down, and a time to build up;

A time to weep, and a time to laugh;
a time to mourn, and a time to dance;

A time to cast away stones,
and a time to gather stones together;
a time to embrace, and a time to refrain from embracing;

A time to get, and a time to lose;
a time to keep, and a time to cast away;

A time to rend, and a time to sew;
a time to keep silence, and a time to speak;

A time to love, and a time to hate;
a time of war, and a time of peace.

What profit hath he that worketh
in that wherein he laboureth?

I have seen the travail,
which God hath given to the sons of men to be exercised in it.

He hath made every thing beautiful in his time:
also he hath set the world in their heart,
so that no man can find out the work that God maketh
from the beginning to the end.

I know that there is no good in them,
but for a man to rejoice, and to do good in his life.

And also that every man should eat and drink,
and enjoy the good of all his labour, it is the gift of God.

I know that, whatsoever God doeth, it shall be for ever:
nothing can be put to it, not any thing taken from it:
and God doeth it, that men should fear before him.

That which hath been is now;
and that which is to be hath already been;
and God requireth that which is past.

And moreover I saw under the sun the place of judgment,
that wickedness was there;
and the place of righteousness, that iniquity was there.

I said in mine heart,
God shall judge the righteous and the wicked:
for there is a time there for every purpose
and for every work.

I said in mine heart concerning the estate of the sons of men,
that God might manifest them,
and that they might see that they themselves are beasts.

For that which befalleth the sons of men befalleth beasts;
even one thing befalleth them:
as the one dieth, so dieth the other;
yea, they have all one breath;
so that a man hath no preeminence above a beast:
for all is vanity.

All go unto one place; all are of the dust,
and all turn to dust again.

Who knoweth the spirit of man that goeth upward,
and the spirit of the beast that goeth downward to the earth?

Wherefore I perceive that there is nothing better,
than that a man should rejoice in his own works;
for that is his portion:
for who shall bring him to see what shall be after him?

Eccles. 11

Cast thy bread upon the waters:
for thou shalt find it after many days.

Give a portion to seven, and also to eight;
for thou knowest not what evil shall be upon the earth.

If the clouds be full of rain,
they empty themselves upon the earth:
and if the tree fall toward the south, or toward the north,
in the place where the tree falleth, there it shall be.

He that observeth the wind shall not sow;
and he that regardeth the clouds shall not reap.

As thou knowest not what is the way of the spirit,
nor how the bones do grow
in the womb of her that is with child:
even so thou knowest not the works of God who maketh all.

In the morning sow thy seed,
and in the evening withhold not thine hand:
for thou knowest not whether shall prosper,
either this or that,
or whether they both shall be alike good.

Truly the light is sweet,
and a pleasant thing it is for the eyes to behold the sun:

But if a man live many years, and rejoice in them all;
yet let him remember the days of darkness;
for they shall be many.
All that cometh is vanity.

Rejoice, O young man, in thy youth;
and let thy heart cheer thee in the days of thy youth,
and walk in the ways of thine heart,
and in the sight of thine eyes:
but know thou, that for all these things
God will bring thee into judgment.

Therefore remove sorrow from thy heart,
and put away evil from thy flesh:
for childhood and youth are vanity.

Eccles. 12:8:14

Vanity of vanities, saith the preacher; all is vanity.

And moreover, because the preacher was wise,
he still taught the people knowledge;
yea, he gave good heed,
and sought out, and set in order many proverbs.

The preacher sought to find out acceptable words:
and that which was written was upright,
even words of truth.

The words of the wise are as goads,
and as nails fastened by the masters of assemblies,
which are given from one shepherd.

And further, by these, my son, be admonished:
of making many books there is no end;
and much study is a weariness of the flesh.

Let us hear the conclusion of the whole matter:
Fear God, and keep his commandments:
for this is the whole duty of man.

For God shall bring every work into judgment,
with every secret thing,
whether it be good, or whether it be evil.

Isaiah

Isaiah 2:2-5

And it shall come to pass in the last days,
that the mountain of the LORD'S house
shall be established in the top of the mountains,
and shall be exalted above the hills;
and all nations shall flow unto it.

And many people shall go up and say,
Come ye, and let us go up to the mountain of the LORD,
to the house of the God of Jacob;
and he will teach us of his ways,
and we will walk in his paths:
for out of Zion shall go forth the law,
and the word of the LORD from Jerusalem.

And he shall judge among the nations,
and shall rebuke many people:

and they shall beat their swords into plowshares,
and their spears into pruninghooks:
nation shall not lift up sword against nation,
neither shall they learn war any more.

O house of Jacob, come ye,
and let us walk in the light of the LORD.

Isaiah 5:20-26

Woe unto them that call evil good, and good evil;
that put darkness for light, and light for darkness;
that put bitter for sweet, and sweet for bitter!

Woe unto them that are wise in their own eyes,
and prudent in their own sight!

Woe unto them that are mighty to drink wine,
and men of strength to mingle strong drink:

Which justify the wicked for reward, and take away
the righteousness of the righteous from him!

Therefore as the fire devoureth the stubble,
and the flame consumeth the chaff,

so their root shall be as rottenness,
and their blossom shall go up as dust:
because they have cast away the law of the LORD of hosts,
and despised the word of the Holy One of Israel.

Therefore is the anger of the LORD kindled against his people,
and he hath stretched forth his hand against them,
and hath smitten them: and the hills did tremble,
and their carcases were torn in the midst of the streets.
For all this his anger is not turned away,
but his hand is stretched out still.

And he will lift up an ensign to the nations from far,
and hiss unto them from the end of the earth:
and, behold, they shall come with speed swiftly:

Isaiah 6

In the year that king Uzziah died
I saw also the Lord sitting upon a throne,
high and lifted up, and his train filled the temple.

Above it stood the seraphims: each one had six wings;
with twain he covered his face,
and with twain he covered his feet,
and with twain he did fly.

And one cried unto another, and said,
Holy, holy, holy, is the LORD of hosts:
the whole earth is full of his glory.

And the posts of the door moved
at the voice of him that cried,
and the house was filled with smoke.

Then said I, Woe is me! for I am undone;
because I am a man of unclean lips,
and I dwell in the midst of a people of unclean lips:
for mine eyes have seen the King, the LORD of hosts.

Then flew one of the seraphims unto me,
having a live coal in his hand,
which he had taken with the tongs from off the altar:

And he laid it upon my mouth, and said,
Lo, this hath touched thy lips;
and thine iniquity is taken away,
and thy sin purged.

Also I heard the voice of the Lord, saying,
Whom shall I send, and who will go for us?
Then said I, Here am I; send me.

And he said, Go, and tell this people,
Hear ye indeed, but understand not;
and see ye indeed, but perceive not.

Make the heart of this people fat,
and make their ears heavy,
and shut their eyes; lest they see with their eyes,
and hear with their ears,
and understand with their heart,
and convert*, and be healed.   *(return)

Then said I, Lord, how long?
And he answered,
Until the cities be wasted without inhabitant,
and the houses without man,
and the land be utterly desolate,

And the LORD have removed men far away,
and there be a great forsaking in the midst of the land.

But yet in it shall be a tenth,
and it shall return, and shall be eaten:
as a teil tree, and as an oak, whose substance is in them,
when they cast their leaves:
so the holy seed shall be the substance thereof.

Isaiah 9:2-7

The people that walked in darkness
have seen a great light:
they that dwell in the land of the shadow of death,
upon them hath the light shined.

Thou hast multiplied the nation, and not increased the joy:
they joy before thee according to the joy in harvest,
and as men rejoice when they divide the spoil.

For thou hast broken the yoke of his burden,
and the staff of his shoulder,
the rod of his oppressor, as in the day of Midian.

For every battle of the warrior is with confused noise,
and garments rolled in blood;
but this shall be with burning and fuel of fire.

For unto us a child is born, unto us a son is given:
and the government shall be upon his shoulder:
and his name shall be called Wonderful, Counsellor,
The mighty God, The everlasting Father,
The Prince of Peace.

Of the increase of his government and peace
there shall be no end,

upon the throne of David, and upon his kingdom,
to order it, and to establish it
with judgment and with justice
from henceforth even for ever.
The zeal of the LORD of hosts will perform this.

Isaiah 9:13-16

For the people turneth not unto him that smiteth them,
neither do they seek the LORD of hosts.

Therefore the LORD will cut off from Israel
head and tail, branch and rush, in one day.

The ancient and honourable, he is the head;
and the prophet that teacheth lies, he is the tail.

For the leaders of this people cause them to err;
and they that are led of them are destroyed.

Isaiah 12

And in that day thou shalt say,
O LORD, I will praise thee:
though thou wast angry with me,
thine anger is turned away,
and thou comfortedst me.

Behold, God is my salvation;
I will trust, and not be afraid:
for the LORD JEHOVAH is my strength and my song;
he also is become my salvation.

Therefore with joy shall ye draw water
out of the wells of salvation.

And in that day shall ye say,
Praise the LORD, call upon his name,
declare his doings among the people,
make mention that his name is exalted.

Sing unto the LORD;
for he hath done excellent things:
this is known in all the earth.

Cry out and shout, thou inhabitant of Zion:
for great is the Holy One of Israel in the midst of thee.

Isaiah 40

Comfort ye, comfort ye my people, saith your God.

Speak ye comfortably to Jerusalem,
and cry unto her,
that her warfare is accomplished,
that her iniquity is pardoned:
for she hath received of the LORD'S hand
double for all her sins.

The voice of him that crieth in the wilderness,
Prepare ye the way of the LORD,
make straight in the desert a highway for our God.

Every valley shall be exalted,
and every mountain and hill shall be made low:
and the crooked shall be made straight,
and the rough places plain:

And the glory of the LORD shall be revealed,
and all flesh shall see it together:
for the mouth of the LORD hath spoken it.

The voice said, Cry.

And he said, What shall I cry?

All flesh is grass, and all the goodliness thereof

is as the flower of the field:

The grass withereth, the flower fadeth:

because the spirit of the LORD bloweth upon it:

surely the people is grass.

The grass withereth, the flower fadeth:

but the word of our God shall stand for ever.

O Zion, that bringest good tidings,

get thee up into the high mountain;

O Jerusalem, that bringest good tidings,

lift up thy voice with strength;

lift it up, be not afraid; say unto the cities of Judah,

Behold your God!

Behold, the Lord God will come with strong hand,

and his arm shall rule for him:

behold, his reward is with him,

and his work before him.

He shall feed his flock like a shepherd:
he shall gather the lambs with his arm,
and carry them in his bosom,
and shall gently lead those that are with young.

Who hath measured the waters in the hollow of his hand,
and meted out heaven with the span,
and comprehended the dust of the earth in a measure,
and weighed the mountains in scales,
and the hills in a balance?

Who hath directed the spirit of the LORD,
or being his counsellor hath taught him?

With whom took he counsel, and who instructed him,
and taught him in the path of judgment,
and taught him knowledge,
and shewed to him the way of understanding?

Behold, the nations are as a drop of a bucket,
and are counted as the small dust of the balance:
behold, he taketh up the isles as a very little thing.

And Lebanon is not sufficient to burn,
nor the beasts thereof sufficient for a burnt offering.

All nations before him are as nothing;
and they are counted to him less than nothing, and vanity.

To whom then will ye liken God?
or what likeness will ye compare unto him?

The workman melteth a graven image,
and the goldsmith spreadeth it over with gold,
and casteth silver chains.

He that is so impoverished that he hath no oblation
chooseth a tree that will not rot;
he seeketh unto him a cunning workman
to prepare a graven image,
that shall not be moved.

Have ye not known? have ye not heard?
hath it not been told you from the beginning?
have ye not understood
from the foundation of the earth?

It is he that sitteth upon the circle of the earth,
and the inhabitants thereof are as grasshoppers;
that stretcheth out the heavens as a curtain,
and spreadeth them out as a tent to dwell in:

That bringeth the princes to nothing;
he maketh the judges of the earth as vanity.

Yea, they shall not be planted;
yea, they shall not be sown:
yea, their stock shall not take root in the earth:
and he shall also blow upon them,
and they shall wither,
and the whirlwind shall take them away as stubble.

To whom then will ye liken me, or shall I be equal?
saith the Holy One.

Lift up your eyes on high,
and behold who hath created these things,
that bringeth out their host by number:
he calleth them all by names
by the greatness of his might,
for that he is strong in power; not one faileth.

Why sayest thou, O Jacob, and speakest, O Israel,
My way is hid from the LORD,
and my judgment is passed over from my God?

Hast thou not known? hast thou not heard,

that the everlasting God, the LORD,

the Creator of the ends of the earth,

fainteth not, neither is weary?

there is no searching of his understanding.

He giveth power to the faint;

and to them that have no might he increaseth strength.

Even the youths shall faint and be weary,

and the young men shall utterly fall:

But they that wait upon the LORD

shall renew their strength;

they shall mount up with wings as eagles;

they shall run, and not be weary;

and they shall walk, and not faint.

Isaiah 42:1-10

Behold my servant, whom I uphold;

mine elect, in whom my soul delighteth;

I have put my spirit upon him:

he shall bring forth judgment to the Gentiles.

He shall not cry, nor lift up,
nor cause his voice to he heard in the street.

A bruised reed shall he not break,
and the smoking flax shall he not quench:
he shall bring forth judgment unto truth.

He shall not fail nor be discouraged,
till he have set judgment in the earth:
and the isles shall wait for his law.

Thus saith God the LORD,
he that created the heavens,
and stretched them out;
he that spread forth the earth,
and that which cometh out of it;
he that giveth breath unto the people upon it,
and spirit to them that walk therein:

I the LORD have called thee in righteousness,
and will hold thine hand, and will keep thee,
and give thee for a covenant of the people,
for a light of the Gentiles;

To open the blind eyes,
to bring out the prisoners from the prison,
and them that sit in darkness out of the prison house.

I am the LORD: that is my name:
and my glory will I not give to another,
neither my praise to graven images.

Behold, the former things are come to pass,
and new things do I declare:
before they spring forth I tell you of them.

Sing unto the LORD a new song,
and his praise from the end of the earth,
ye that go down to the sea, and all that is therein;
the isles, and the inhabitants thereof.

Isaiah 42:18-25

Hear, ye deaf; and look, ye blind, that ye may see.

Who is blind, but my servant?
or deaf, as my messenger that I sent?
who is blind as he that is perfect,
and blind as the LORD'S servant?

Seeing many things, but thou observest not;
opening the ears, but he heareth not.

The LORD is well pleased for his righteousness' sake;
he will magnify the law, and make it honourable.

But this is a people robbed and spoiled;
they are all of them snared in holes,
and they are hid in prison houses:
they are for a prey, and none delivereth;
for a spoil, and none saith, Restore.

Who among you will give ear to this?
who will hearken and hear for the time to come?

Who gave Jacob for a spoil, and Israel to the robbers?
did not the LORD, he against whom we have sinned?
for they would not walk in his ways,
neither were they obedient unto his law.

Therefore he hath poured upon him the fury of his anger,
and the strength of battle:
and it hath set him on fire round about,
yet he knew not; and it burned him, yet he laid it not to heart.

Isaiah 49:1-10

Listen, O isles, unto me;
and hearken, ye people, from far;
The LORD hath called me from the womb;
from the bowels of my mother
hath he made mention of my name.

And he hath made my mouth like a sharp sword;
in the shadow of his hand hath he hid me,
and made me a polished shaft;
in his quiver hath he hid me;

And said unto me, Thou art my servant, O Israel,
in whom I will be glorified.

Then I said, I have laboured in vain,
I have spent my strength for nought, and in vain:
yet surely my judgment is with the LORD,
and my work with my God.

And now, saith the LORD
that formed me from the womb to be his servant,
to bring Jacob again to him,
Though Israel be not gathered,
yet shall I be glorious in the eyes of the LORD,
and my God shall be my strength.

And he said,

It is a light thing that thou shouldest be my servant

to raise up the tribes of Jacob,

and to restore the preserved of Israel:

I will also give thee for a light to the Gentiles,

that thou mayest be my salvation unto the end of the earth.

Thus saith the LORD,

the Redeemer of Israel, and his Holy One,

to him whom man despiseth,

to him whom the nation abhoreth,

to a servant of rulers, Kings shall see and arise,

princes also shall worship,

because of the LORD that is faithful,

and the Holy One of Israel,

and he shall choose thee.

Thus saith the LORD,

In an acceptable time have I heard thee,

and in a day of salvation have I helped thee:

and I will preserve thee,

and give thee for a covenant of the people,

to establish the earth,

to cause to inherit the desolate heritages;

That thou mayest say to the prisoners, Go forth;
to them that are in darkness, Shew yourselves.
They shall feed in the ways,
and their pastures shall be in all high places.

They shall not hunger nor thirst;
neither shall the heat nor sun smite them:
for he that hath mercy on them shall lead them,
even by the springs of water shall he guide them.

Isaiah 52:7-15

How beautiful upon the mountains
are the feet of him that bringeth good tidings,
that publisheth peace; that bringeth good tidings of good,
that publisheth salvation;
that saith unto Zion, Thy God reigneth!

Thy watchmen shall lift up the voice;
with the voice together shall they sing:
for they shall see eye to eye,
when the LORD shall bring again Zion.

Break forth into joy, sing together,
ye waste places of Jerusalem:
for the LORD hath comforted his people,
he hath redeemed Jerusalem.

The LORD hath made bare his holy arm
in the eyes of all the nations;
and all the ends of the earth
shall see the salvation of our God.

Depart ye, depart ye, go ye out from thence,
touch no unclean thing;
go ye out of the midst of her;
be ye clean, that bear the vessels of the LORD.

For ye shall not go out with haste, nor go by flight:
for the LORD will go before you;
and the God of Israel will be your rereward.

Behold, my servant shall deal prudently,
he shall be exalted and extolled,
and be very high.

As many were astonied at thee;
his visage was so marred more than any man,
and his form more than the sons of men:

So shall he sprinkle many nations;
the kings shall shut their mouths at him:
for that which had not been told them shall they see;
and that which they had not heard shall they consider.

Isaiah 53

Who hath believed our report?
and to whom is the arm of the LORD revealed?

For he shall grow up before him as a tender plant,
and as a root out of a dry ground:
he hath no form nor comeliness;
and when we shall see him,
there is no beauty that we should desire him.

He is despised and rejected of men;
a man of sorrows, and acquainted with grief:
and we hid as it were our faces from him;
he was despised, and we esteemed him not.

Surely he hath borne our griefs, and carried our sorrows:
yet we did esteem him stricken,
smitten of God, and afflicted.

But he was wounded for our transgressions,
he was bruised for our iniquities:
the chastisement of our peace was upon him;
and with his stripes we are healed.

All we like sheep have gone astray;
we have turned every one to his own way;
and the LORD hath laid on him the iniquity of us all.

He was oppressed, and he was afflicted,
yet he opened not his mouth:
he is brought as a lamb to the slaughter,
and as a sheep before her shearers is dumb,
so he openeth not his mouth.

He was taken from prison and from judgment:
and who shall declare his generation?
for he was cut off out of the land of the living:
for the transgression of my people was he stricken.

And he made his grave with the wicked,
and with the rich in his death;
because he had done no violence,
neither was any deceit in his mouth.

Yet it pleased the LORD to bruise him;
he hath put him to grief:
when thou shalt make his soul an offering for sin,
he shall see his seed, he shall prolong his days,
and the pleasure of the LORD shall prosper in his hand.

He shall see of the travail of his soul,
and shall be satisfied:
by his knowledge shall my righteous servant justify many;
for he shall bear their iniquities.

Therefore will I divide him a portion with the great,
and he shall divide the spoil with the strong;
because he hath poured out his soul unto death:
and he was numbered with the transgressors;
and he bare the sin of many,
and made intercession for the transgressors.

Isaiah 55

Ho, every one that thirsteth,
come ye to the waters,
and he that hath no money;
come ye, buy, and eat;
come, buy wine and milk without money
and without price.

Wherefore do you spend money
for that which is not bread?
and your labour for that which satisfieth not?
hearken diligently unto me,
and eat ye that which is good,
and let your soul delight itself in fatness.

Incline your ear, and come unto me:
hear, and your soul shall live;
and I will make an everlasting covenant with you,
even the sure mercies of David.

Behold, I have given him for a witness to the people,
a leader and commander to the people.

Behold, thou shalt call a nation
that thou knowest not,
and nations that knew not thee shall run unto thee
because of the LORD thy God,
and for the Holy One of Israel;
for he hath glorified thee.

Seek ye the LORD while he may be found,
call ye upon him while he is near:

Let the wicked forsake his way,
and the unrighteous man his thoughts:
and let him return unto the LORD,
and he will have mercy upon him;
and to our God, for he will abundantly pardon.

For my thoughts are not your thoughts,
neither are your ways my ways, saith the LORD.

For as the heavens are higher than the earth,
so are my ways higher than your ways,
and my thoughts than your thoughts.

For as the rain cometh down,
and the snow from heaven,
and returneth not thither, but watereth the earth,
and maketh it bring forth and bud,
that it may give seed to the sower,
and bread to the eater:

So shall my word be that goeth forth out of my mouth:
it shall not return unto me void,
but it shall accomplish that which I please,
and it shall prosper in the thing whereto I sent it.

For ye shall go out with joy, and be led forth with peace:
the mountains and the hills
shall break forth before you into singing,
and all the trees of the field shall clap their hands.

Instead of the thorn shall come up the fir tree,
and instead of the brier shall come up the myrtle tree:
and it shall be to the LORD for a name,
for an everlasting sign that shall not be cut off.

Isaiah 56:6-8

Also the sons of the stranger,
that join themselves to the LORD,
to serve him, and to love the name of the LORD,
to be his servants,
every one that keepeth the sabbath from polluting it,
and taketh hold of my covenant;

Even them will I bring to my holy mountain,
and make them joyful in my house of prayer:
their burnt offerings and their sacrifices
shall be accepted upon mine alter;
for mine house shall be called
an house of prayer for all people.

The Lord God which gathereth
the outcasts of Israel saith,
Yet will I gather others to him,
besides those that are gathered unto him.

Isaiah 60:1-5

Arise, shine; for thy light is come,
and the glory of the LORD is risen upon thee.

For, behold, the darkness shall cover the earth,
and gross darkness the people:
but the LORD shall arise upon thee,
and his glory shall be seen upon thee.

And the Gentiles shall come to thy light,
and kings to the brightness of thy rising.

Lift up thine eyes round about, and see:
all they gather themselves together,
they come to thee: thy sons shall come from far,
and thy daughters shall be nursed at thy side.

Then thou shalt see, and flow together,
and thine heart shall fear, and be enlarged;
because the abundance of the sea
shall be converted unto thee,
the forces of the Gentiles shall come unto thee.

Isaiah 61

The spirit of the Lord GOD is upon me;
because the LORD hath anointed me
to preach good tidings unto the meek;
he hath sent me to bind up the brokenhearted,
to proclaim liberty to the captives,
and the opening of the prison to them that are bound;

To proclaim the acceptable year of the LORD,
and the day of vengeance of our God;
to comfort all that mourn;

To appoint unto them that mourn in Zion,
to give unto them beauty for ashes,
the oil of joy for mourning,
the garment of praise for the spirit of heaviness;
that they might be called trees of righteousness,
the planting of the LORD,
that he might be glorified.

And they shall build the old wastes,
they shall raise up the former desolations,
and they shall repair the waste cities,
the desolations of many generations.

And strangers shall stand and feed your flocks,
and the sons of the alien
shall be your plowmen and your vinedressers.

But ye shall be named the Priests of the LORD:
men shall call you the Ministers of our God:
ye shall eat the riches of the Gentiles,
and in their glory shall ye boast yourselves.

For your shame ye shall have double;
and for confusion they shall rejoice in their portion:
therefore in their land they shall possess the double:
everlasting joy shall be unto them.

For I the LORD love judgment,
I hate robbery for burnt offering;
and I will direct their work in truth,
and I will make an everlasting covenant with them.

And their seed shall be known among the Gentiles,
and their offspring among the people:
all that see them shall acknowledge them,
that they are the seed which the LORD hath blessed.

I will greatly rejoice in the LORD,
my soul shall be joyful in my God;
for he hath clothed me with the garments of salvation,
he hath covered me with the robe of righteousness,
as a bridegroom decketh himself with ornaments,
and as a bride adorneth herself with her jewels.

For as the earth bringeth forth her bud,
and as the garden causeth the things
that are sown in it to spring forth;
so the Lord GOD will cause righteousness and praise
to spring forth before all the nations.

Isaiah 66:21-24

A nd I will also take of them for priests and for Levites,
saith the LORD.

For as the new heavens and the new earth,
which I will make,
shall remain before me, saith the LORD,
so shall your seed and your name remain.

And it shall come to pass,
that from one new moon to another,
and from one sabbath to another,
shall all flesh come to worship before me, saith the LORD.

And they shall go forth,
and look upon the carcases of the men
that have transgressed against me:
for their worm shall not die,
neither shall their fire be quenched;
and they shall be an abhorring unto all flesh.

Jeremiah

Jeremiah 9:23-24

Thus saith the LORD,
   Let not the wise man glory in his wisdom,
neither let the mighty man glory in his might,
let not the rich man glory in his riches:

But let him that glorieth glory in this,
that he understandeth and knoweth me,
that I am the LORD which exercise
lovingkindness, judgment, and righteousness,
in the earth:
for in these things I delight, saith the LORD.

Jeremiah 17:5-14

Thus saith the LORD;
   Cursed be the man that trusteth in man,
and maketh flesh his arm,
and whose heart departeth from the LORD.

For he shall be like the heath in the desert,
and shall not see when good cometh;
but shall inhabit the parched places in the wilderness,
in a salt land and not inhabited.

Blessed is the man that trusteth in the LORD,
and whose hope the LORD is.

For he shall be as a tree planted by the waters,
and that spreadeth out her roots by the river,
and shall not see when heat cometh,
but her leaf shall be green;
and shall not be careful in the year of drought,
neither shall cease from yielding fruit.

The heart is deceitful above all things,
and desperately wicked: who can know it?

I the LORD search the heart, I try the reins,

even to give every man according to his ways,

and according to the fruit of his doings.

As the partridge sitteth on eggs, and hatcheth them not;

so he that getteth riches, and not by right,

shall leave them in the midst of his days,

and at his end shall be a fool.

A glorious high throne from the beginning

is the place of our sanctuary.

O LORD, the hope of Israel,

all that forsake thee shall be ashamed,

and they that depart from me shall be written in the earth,

because they have forsaken the LORD,

the fountain of living waters.

Heal me, O LORD, and I shall be healed;

save me, and I shall be saved:

for thou art my praise.

Jeremiah 31:31-34

Behold, the days come, saith the LORD,
that I will make a new covenant with the house of Israel,
and with the house of Judah:

Not according to the covenant that I made with their fathers
in the day that I took them by the hand
to bring them out of the land of Egypt;
which my covenant they brake,
although I was an husband unto them, saith the LORD:

But this shall be the covenant that I will make
with the house of Israel;
After those days, saith the LORD,
I will put my law in their inward parts,
and write it in their hearts;
and will be their God, and they shall be my people.

And they shall teach no more every man his neighbour,
and every man his brother, saying, Know the LORD:
for they shall all know me,
from the least of them unto the greatest of them,
saith the LORD:
for I will forgive their iniquity,
and I will remember their sin no more.

Jeremiah 33:3

Call unto me, and I will answer thee, and shew thee great and mighty things, which thou knowest not.

Matthew

Matthew 4:23-25

And Jesus went about all Galilee,
teaching in their synagogues,
and preaching the gospel of the kingdom,
and healing all manner of sickness
and all manner of disease among the people.

And his fame went throughout all Syria:
and they brought unto him all sick people
that were taken with divers diseases and torments,
and those which were possessed with devils,
and those which were lunatic,
and those that had the palsy;
and he healed them.

And there followed him great multitudes of people
from Galilee, and from Decapolis,
and from Jerusalem, and from Judaea,
and from beyond Jordan.

Matthew 5:1-19

And seeing the multitudes,
he went up into a mountain:
and when he was set, his disciples came unto him:

And he opened his mouth, and taught them, saying,

Blessed are the poor in spirit:
for theirs is the kingdom of heaven.

Blessed are they that mourn:
for they shall be comforted.

Blessed are the meek:
for they shall inherit the earth.

Blessed are they
which do hunger and thirst after righteousness:
for they shall be filled.

Blessed are the merciful:
for they shall obtain mercy.

Blessed are the pure in heart:
for they shall see God.

Blessed are the peacemakers:
for they shall be called the children of God.

Blessed are they
which are persecuted for righteousness' sake:
for theirs is the kingdom of heaven.

Blessed are ye,
when men shall revile you, and persecute you,
and shall say all manner of evil against you falsely,
for my sake.

Rejoice, and be exceeding glad:
for great is your reward in heaven:
for so persecuted they the prophets
which were before you.

Ye are the salt of the earth:
but if the salt have lost his savour,
wherewith shall it be salted?
it is thenceforth good for nothing,
but to be cast out,
and to be trodden under foot of men.

Ye are the light of the world.
A city that is set on an hill cannot be hid.

Neither do men light a candle,
and put it under a bushel,
but on a candlestick;
and it giveth light unto all that are in the house.

Let your light so shine before men,
that they may see your good works,
and glorify your Father which is in heaven.

Think not that I am come
to destroy the law*, or the prophets:
I am not come to destroy, but to fulfil.

For verily I say unto you,
Till heaven and earth pass,
one jot or one tittle shall in no wise pass from the law,
till all be fulfilled.

Whosoever therefore shall break
one of these least commandments,
and shall teach men so,
he shall be called the least in the kingdom of heaven:
but whosoever shall do and teach them,
the same shall be called great in the kingdom of heaven.

law* - The Greek word here is *nomos*, which means law. But in the context
of saying, "the law, or the prophets", the Hebrew way of saying this would
be to say, "the Torah, or the Prophets", as these are the first two sections of
the Hebrew Bible. Because there is no Greek word that completely translates
torah, we see the same limitations in the Greek that we have in English. For
this reason, I always choose to simply say *torah* whenever I repeat this verse.

Matthew 6:19-24

Lay not up for yourselves treasures upon earth,
where moth and rust doth corrupt,
and where thieves break through and steal:

But lay up for yourselves treasures in heaven,
where neither moth nor rust doth corrupt,
and where thieves do not break through nor steal:

For where your treasure is,
there will your heart be also.

The light of the body is the eye:
if therefore thine eye be single,
thy whole body shall be full of light.

But if thine eye be evil,
thy whole body shall be full of darkness.
If therefore the light that is in thee be darkness,
how great is that darkness!

No man can serve two masters:
for either he will hate the one, and love the other;
or else he will hold to the one, and despise the other.
Ye cannot serve God and mam-mon*.   *(riches)

Matthew 6:31-34

Therefore take no thought, saying,
   What shall we eat? or, What shall we drink? or,
Wherewithal shall we be clothed?

(For after all these things do the Gentiles seek:)
for your heavenly Father knoweth
that ye have need of all these things.

But seek ye first the kingdom of God,
and his righteousness;
and all these things shall be added unto you.

Take therefore no thought for the morrow:
for the morrow shall take thought
for the things of itself.
Sufficient unto the day is the evil thereof.

Matthew 7

Judge not, that ye be not judged.

For with what judgment ye judge, ye shall be judged:
and with what measure ye mete,
it shall be measured to you again.

And why beholdest thou the mote
that is in thy brother's eye, but considerest not
the beam that is in thine own eye?

Or how wilt thou say to thy brother,
Let me pull out the mote out of thine eye;
and, behold, a beam is in thine own eye?

Thou hypocrite,

first cast out the beam out of thine own eye;

and then shalt thou see clearly

to cast out the mote out of thy brother's eye.

Give not that which is holy unto the dogs,

neither cast ye your pearls before swine,

lest they trample them under their feet,

and turn again and rend you.

Ask, and it shall be given you;

seek, and ye shall find;

knock, and it shall be opened unto you:

For every one that asketh receiveth;

and he that seeketh findeth;

and to him that knocketh it shall be opened.

Or what man is there of you,

whom if his son ask bread, will he give him a stone?

Or if he ask a fish, will he give him a serpent?

If ye then, being evil,
know how to give good gifts unto your children,
how much more shall your Father which is in heaven
give good things to them that ask him?

Therefore all things whatsoever ye would
that men should do to you,
do ye even so to them:
for this is the law and the prophets.

Enter ye in at the strait gate:
for wide is the gate, and broad is the way,
that leadeth to destruction,
and many there be which go in thereat:

Because strait is the gate, and narrow is the way,
which leadeth unto life,
and few there be that find it.

Beware of false prophets,
which come to you in sheep's clothing,
but inwardly they are ravening wolves.

Ye shall know them by their fruits.
Do men gather grapes of thorns,
or figs of thistles?

Even so every good tree bringeth forth good fruit;
but a corrupt tree bringeth forth evil fruit.

A good tree cannot bring forth evil fruit,
neither can a corrupt tree bring forth good fruit.

Every tree that bringeth not forth good fruit
is hewn down, and cast into the fire.

Wherefore by their fruits ye shall know them.

Not every one that saith unto me, Lord, Lord,
shall enter into the kingdom of heaven;
but he that doeth the will of my Father which is in heaven.

Many will say to me in that day,
Lord, Lord, have we not prophesied in thy name?
and in thy name have cast out devils?
and in thy name done many wonderful works?

And then will I profess unto them, I never knew you:
depart from me, ye that work iniquity*.

Therefore whosoever heareth these sayings of mine,
and doeth them,
I will liken him unto a wise man,
which built his house upon a rock:

And the rain descended, and the floods came,
and the winds blew,
and beat upon that house; and it fell not:
for it was founded upon a rock.

And every one that heareth these sayings of mine,
and doeth them not,
shall be likened unto a foolish man,
which built his house upon the sand:

And the rain descended, and the floods came,
and the winds blew,
and beat upon that house;
and it fell: and great was the fall of it.

And it came to pass,
when Jesus had ended these sayings,
the people were astonished at his doctrine:

For he taught them as one having authority,
and not as the scribes.

*iniquity – The Greek word here is *anomia*, which is the opposite of *nomos*, which
means "law". *Anomia*, therefore, means against the law, anti-law, or lawlessness.

Matthew 13

The same day went Jesus out of the house,
and sat by the sea side.

And great multitudes were gathered together unto him,
so that he went into a ship, and sat;
and the whole multitude stood on the shore.

And he spake many things unto them in parables, saying,
Behold, a sower went forth to sow;

And when he sowed, some seeds fell by the way side,
and the fowls came and devoured them up:

Some fell upon stony places, where they had not much earth:
and forthwith they sprung up,
because they had no deepness of earth:

And when the sun was up, they were scorched;
and because they had no root, they withered away.

And some fell among thorns;
and the thorns sprung up, and choked them:

But other fell into good ground, and brought forth fruit,
some an hundredfold, some sixtyfold, some thirtyfold.

Who hath ears to hear, let him hear.

And the disciples came, and said unto him,
Why speakest thou unto them in parables?

He answered and said unto them,
Because it is given unto you
to know the mysteries of the kingdom of heaven,
but to them it is not given.

For whosoever hath, to him shall be given,
and he shall have more abundance:
but whosoever hath not,
from him shall be taken away even that he hath.

Therefore speak I to them in parables:
because they seeing see not;
and hearing they hear not,
neither do they understand.

And in them is fulfilled the prophecy of Esaias*,   *(Isaiah)
which saith, By hearing ye shall hear,
and shall not understand;
and seeing ye shall see, and shall not perceive:

For this people's heart is waxed gross,
and their ears are dull of hearing,
and their eyes they have closed;
lest at any time they should see with their eyes,
and hear with their ears,
and should understand with their heart,
and should be converted*, *(return)
and I should heal them.

But blessed are your eyes, for they see:
and your ears, for they hear.

For verily I say unto you,
That many prophets and righteous men
have desired to see those things which ye see,
and have not seen them;
and to hear those things which ye hear
and have not heard them.

Hear ye therefore the parable of the sower.

When any one heareth the word of the kingdom,
and understandeth it not,
then cometh the wicked one,
and catcheth away that which was sown in his heart.
This is he which received seed by the way side.

But he that received the seed into stony places,
the same is he that heareth the word,
and anon with joy receiveth it;

Yet hath he not root in himself, but dureth for a while:
for when tribulation or persecution
ariseth because of the word,
by and by he is offended.

He also that received seed among the thorns
is he that heareth the word;
and the care of this world,
and the deceitfulness of riches,
choke the word, and he becometh unfruitful.

But he that received seed into the good ground
is he that heareth the word,
and understandeth it;
which also beareth fruit, and bringeth forth
some an hundredfold, some sixty, some thirty.

Another parable put he forth unto them, saying,
The kingdom of heaven is likened unto a man
which sowed good seed in his field:

But while men slept, his enemy came
and sowed tares* among the wheat,   *(weeds)
and went his way.

But when the blade was sprung up,
and brought forth fruit,
then appeared the tares also.

So the servants of the householder came and said unto him,
Sir, didst not thou sow good seed in thy field?
from whence then hath it tares?

He said unto them, An enemy hath done this.
The servants said unto him,
Wilt thou then that we go and gather them up?

But he said, Nay; lest while ye gather up the tares,
ye root up also the wheat with them.

Let both grow together until the harvest:
and in the time of the harvest I will say to the reapers,
Gather ye together first the tares,
and bind them in bundles to burn them:
but gather the wheat into my barn.

Another parable put he forth unto them, saying,

The kingdom of heaven is like to a grain of mustard seed,
which a man took, and sowed in his field:

Which indeed is the least of all seeds:
but when it is grown, it is the greatest among herbs,
and becometh a tree,
so that the birds of the air come
and lodge in the branches thereof.

Another parable spake he unto them;
The kingdom of heaven is like unto leaven,
which a woman took, and hid in three measures of meal,
till the whole was leavened.

All these things spake Jesus unto the multitude in parables;
and without a parable spake he not unto them:

That it might be fulfilled
which was spoken by the prophet, saying,
I will open my mouth in parables;
I will utter things which have been kept secret
from the foundation of the world.

Then Jesus sent the multitude away,
and went into the house:
and his disciples came unto him, saying,
Declare unto us the parable of the tares of the field.

He answered and said unto them,
He that soweth the good seed is the Son of man;

The field is the world;
the good seed are the children of the kingdom;
but the tares are the children of the wicked one;

The enemy that sowed them is the devil;
the harvest is the end of the world;
and the reapers are the angels.

As therefore the tares are gathered and burned in the fire;
so shall it be in the end of this world.

The Son of man shall send forth his angels,
and they shall gather out of his kingdom all things that offend,
and them which do iniquity*; *(lawlessness)

And shall cast them into a furnace of fire:
there shall be wailing and gnashing of teeth.

Then shall the righteous shine forth
as the sun in the kingdom of their Father.
Who hath ears to hear, let him hear.

Again, the kingdom of heaven
is like unto treasure hid in a field;
the which when a man hath found, he hideth,
and for joy thereof goeth and selleth
all that he hath, and buyeth that field.

Again, the kingdom of heaven is like unto a merchant man,
seeking goodly pearls:

Who, when he had found one pearl of great price,
went and sold all that he had, and bought it.

Again, the kingdom of heaven is like unto a net,
that was cast into the sea, and gathered of every kind:

Which, when it was full, they drew to shore,
and sat down, and gathered the good into vessels,
but cast the bad away.

So shall it be at the end of the world:
the angels shall come forth,
and sever the wicked from among the just,

And shall cast them into the furnace of fire:
there shall be wailing and gnashing of teeth.

Jesus saith unto them,
Have ye understood all these things?
They say unto him, Yea, Lord.

Then said he unto them, Therefore every scribe
which is instructed unto the kingdom of heaven
is like unto a man that is an householder,
which bringeth forth out of his treasure things new and old.

And it came to pass,
that when Jesus had finished these parables,
he departed thence.

And when he was come into his own country,
he taught them in their synagogue,
insomuch that they were astonished, and said,
Whence hath this man this wisdom,
and these mighty works?

Is not this the carpenter's son?
is not his mother called Mary?
and his brethren, James, and Joses, and Simon, and Judas?

And his sisters, are they not all with us?
Whence then hath this man all these things?

And they were offended in him. But Jesus said unto them,
A prophet is not without honour,
save in his own country, and in his own house.

And he did not many mighty works there
because of their unbelief.

Matthew 25:31-46

When the Son of man shall come in his glory,
and all the holy angels with him,
then shall he sit upon the throne of his glory:

And before him shall be gathered all nations:
and he shall separate them one from another,
as a shepherd divideth his sheep from the goats:

And he shall set the sheep on his right hand,
but the goats on the left.

Then shall the King say unto them on his right hand,
Come, ye blessed of my Father,
inherit the kingdom prepared for you
from the foundation of the world:

For I was an hungered, and ye gave me meat:
I was thirsty, and ye gave me drink:
I was a stranger, and ye took me in:

Naked, and ye clothed me:
I was sick, and ye visited me:
I was in prison, and ye came unto me.

Then shall the righteous answer him, saying,
Lord, when saw we thee an hungered, and fed thee?
or thirsty, and gave thee drink?

When saw we thee a stranger, and took thee in?
or naked, and clothed thee?

Or when saw we thee sick, or in prison, and came unto thee?

And the King shall answer and say unto them,
Verily I say unto you, Inasmuch as ye have done it
unto one of the least of these my brethren,
ye have done it unto me.

Then shall he say also unto them on the left hand,
Depart from me, ye cursed, into everlasting fire,
prepared for the devil and his angels:

For I was an hungered, and ye gave me no meat:
I was thirsty, and ye gave me no drink:

I was a stranger, and ye took me not in:
naked, and ye clothed me not:
sick, and in prison, and ye visited me not.

Then shall they also answer him, saying,
Lord, when saw we thee an hungered, or athirst,
or a stranger, or naked, or sick, or in prison,
and did not minister unto thee?

Then shall he answer them, saying,
Verily I say unto you,
Inasmuch as ye did it not to one of the least of these,
ye did it not to me.

And these shall go away into everlasting punishment:
but the righteous into life eternal.

Matthew 28:18-20

And Jesus came and spake unto them, saying,
All power is given unto me in heaven and in earth.

Go ye therefore, and teach all nations,
baptizing them in the name of the Father,
and of the Son, and of the Holy Ghost*:   *(Spirit)

Teaching them to observe all things
whatsoever I have commanded you:
and, lo, I am with you alway,
even unto the end of the world. Amen

*Ghost – The Greek word here is *pneuma*. Throughout the KJV this is usually translated as "spirit". It can also mean "wind" or "breath". In John 4:24 Jesus states, "God is a *pneuma*." The translators chose "Spirit" rather than "Ghost". To define anything pertaining to God as a "ghost" seems completely inappropriate, especially to our modern definition of what a ghost implies. So I always choose to substitute "Spirit" whenever I see "Ghost" in the KJV.

Mark

Mark 1:14-18

Now after that John was put in prison,
Jesus came into Galilee,
preaching the gospel of the kingdom of God,

And saying, The time is fulfilled,
and the kingdom of God is at hand:
repent ye, and believe the gospel.

Now as he walked by the sea of Galilee,
he saw Simon and Andrew his brother
casting a net into the sea: for they were fishers.

And Jesus said unto them, Come ye after me,
and I will make you to become fishers of men.

And straightway they forsook their nets, and followed him.

Mark 2:16-17

And when the scribes and Pharisees
saw him eat with publicans and sinners,
they said unto his disciples,
How is it that he eateth and drinketh
with publicans and sinners?

When Jesus heard it, he saith unto them,
They that are whole have no need of the physician,
but they that are sick:
I came not to call the righteous, but sinners to repentance.

Mark 3:1-6

And he entered again into the synagogue;
and there was a man there which had a withered hand.

And they watched him,
whether he would heal him on the sabbath day;
that they might accuse him.

And he saith unto the man which had the withered hand,
Stand forth.

And he saith unto them,

Is it lawful to do good on the sabbath days, or to do evil?

to save life, or to kill? But they held their peace.

And when he had looked round about on them with anger,

being grieved for the hardness of their hearts,

he saith unto the man, Stretch forth thine hand.

And he stretched it out:

and his hand was restored whole as the other.

And the Pharisees went forth,

and straightway took counsel with the Herodians against him,

how they might destroy him.

Mark 8:34-38

And when he had called the people unto him
with his disciples also, he said unto them,

Whosoever will come after me, let him deny himself,

and take up his cross, and follow me.

For whosoever will save his life shall lose it;

but whosoever shall lose his life for my sake and the gospel's,

the same shall save it.

For what shall it profit a man,

if he shall gain the whole world, and lose his own soul?

Or what shall a man give in exchange for his soul?

Whosoever therefore shall be ashamed of me
and of my words
in this adulterous and sinful generation;
of him also shall the Son of man be ashamed,
when he cometh in the glory of his Father
with the holy angels.

Mark 10:13-15

And they brought young children to him,
that he should touch them:
and his disciples rebuked those that brought them.

But when Jesus saw it, he was much displeased,
and said unto them,
Suffer the little children to come unto me,
and forbid them not: for of such is the kingdom of God.

Verily I say unto you,
Whosoever shall not receive the kingdom of God
as a little child, he shall not enter therein.

Mark 11:22-26

And Jesus answering saith unto them, Have faith in God.

For verily I say unto you,
That whosoever shall say unto this mountain,
Be thou removed, and be thou cast into the sea;
and shall not doubt in his heart,
but shall believe that those things which he saith
shall come to pass; he shall have whatsoever he saith.

Therefore I say unto you,
What things soever ye desire, when ye pray,
believe that ye receive them, and ye shall have them.

And when ye stand praying, forgive,
if ye have aught against any:
that your Father also which is in heaven
may forgive you your trespasses.

But if ye do not forgive,
neither will your Father which is in heaven
forgive your trespasses.

Mark 12:24-31

And Jesus answering said unto them,
Do ye not therefore err,
because ye know not the scriptures,
neither the power of God?

For when they shall rise from the dead,
they neither marry, nor are given in marriage;
but are as the angels which are in heaven.

And as touching the dead, that they rise:
have ye not read in the book of Moses,
how in the bush God spake unto him, saying,
I am the God of Abraham, and the God of Isaac,
and the God of Jacob?

He is not the God of the dead, but the God of the living:
ye therefore do greatly err.

And one of the scribes came,
and having heard them reasoning together,
and perceiving that he had answered them well, asked him,
Which is the first commandment of all?

And Jesus answered him,

The first of all the commandments is,

Hear, O Israel; the Lord our God is one Lord:

And thou shalt love the Lord thy God with all thy heart,

and with all thy soul, and with all thy mind,

and with all thy strength:

this is the first commandment.

And the second is like, namely this,

Thou shalt love thy neighbour as thyself.

There is none other commandment greater than these.

Mark 16:15-20

And he said unto them, Go ye into all the world,
and preach the gospel to every creature.

He that believeth and is baptized shall be saved;

but he that believeth not shall be damned.

And these signs shall follow them that believe;

In my name shall they cast out devils;

they shall speak with new tongues;

They shall take up serpents;

and if they drink any deadly thing, it shall not hurt them;

they shall lay hands on the sick, and they shall recover.

So then after the Lord had spoken unto them,

he was received up into heaven,

and sat on the right hand of God.

And they went forth, and preached every where,

the Lord working with them,

and confirming the word with signs following. Amen.

John

John 1:1-24

In the beginning was the Word,
and the Word was with God,
and the Word was God.

The same was in the beginning with God.

All things were made by him;
and without him was not anything made that was made.

In him was life; and the life was the light of men.

And the light shineth in darkness;
and the darkness comprehended it not.

There was a man sent from God,
whose name was John.

The same came for a witness,
to bear witness of the Light,
that all men through him might believe.

He was not that Light,
but was sent to bear witness of that Light.

That was the true Light,
which lighteth every man that cometh into the world.

He was in the world, and the world was made by him,
and the world knew him not.

He came unto his own, and his own received him not.

But as many as received him,
to them gave he power to become the sons of God,
even to them that believe on his name:

Which were born, not of blood,
nor of the will of the flesh, nor of the will of man,
but of God.

And the Word was made flesh, and dwelt among us,
(and we beheld his glory,
the glory as of the only begotten of the Father,)
full of grace and truth.

John bare witness of him, and cried, saying,
This was he of whom I spake,
He that cometh after me is preferred before me:
for he was before me.

And of his fulness have all we received,
and grace for grace.

For the law was given by Moses,
but grace and truth came by Jesus Christ.

No man hath seen God at any time;
the only begotten Son,
which is in the bosom of the Father,
he hath declared him.

And this is the record of John,
when the Jews sent priests and Levites
from Jerusalem to ask him,
Who art thou?

And he confessed, and denied not; but confessed,
I am not the Christ.

And they asked him, What then?
Art thou Elias*? *(Elijah)

And he saith, I am not.

Art thou that prophet? And he answered, No.

Then said they unto him, Who art thou?

that we may give an answer to them that sent us.

What sayest thou of thyself?

He said, I am the voice of one crying in the wilderness,

Make straight the way of the Lord,

as said the prophet Esaias*.   *(Isaiah)

And they which were sent were of the Pharisees.

John 1:29-34

The next day John seeth Jesus coming unto him,
    and saith,

Behold the Lamb of God,

which taketh away the sin of the world.

This is he of whom I said,

After me cometh a man which is preferred before me:

for he was before me.

And I knew him not:

but that he should be made manifest to Israel,

therefore am I come baptizing with water.

And John bare record, saying,

I saw the Spirit descending from heaven like a dove,

and it abode upon him.

And I knew him not:

but he that sent me to baptize with water,

the same said unto me,

Upon whom thou shalt see the Spirit descending,

and remaining on him,

the same is he which baptizeth with the Holy Ghost.

And I saw, and bare record that this is the Son of God.

John 3:1-21

There was a man of the Pharisees, named Nicodemus,
a ruler of the Jews:

The same came to Jesus by night, and said unto him,

Rabbi, we know that thou art a teacher come from God:

for no man can do these miracles that thou doest,

except God be with him.

Jesus answered and said unto him,
Verily, verily I say unto thee,
Except a man be born again,
he cannot see the kingdom of God.

Nicodemus saith unto him,
How can a man be born when he is old?
can he enter the second time into his mother's womb,
and be born?

Jesus answered, Verily, verily, I say unto thee,
Except a man be born of water and of the Spirit,
he cannot enter into the kingdom of God.

That which is born of the flesh is flesh;
and that which is born of the Spirit is spirit.

Marvel not that I said unto thee,
Ye must be born again.

The wind bloweth where it listeth,
and thou hearest the sound thereof,
but canst not tell whence it cometh,
and whither it goeth:
so is every one that is born of the Spirit.

Nicodemus answered and said unto him,
How can these things be?

Jesus answered and said unto him,
Art thou a master of Israel,
and knowest not these things?

Verily, verily, I say unto thee,
We speak that we do know,
and testify that we have seen;
and ye receive not our witness.

If I have told you earthly things,
and ye believe not, how shall ye believe,
if I tell you of heavenly things?

And no man hath ascended up to heaven,
but he that came down from heaven,
even the Son of man which is in heaven.

And as Moses lifted up the serpent in the wilderness,
even so must the Son of man be lifted up:

That whosoever believeth in him
should not perish, but have eternal life.

For God so loved the world,
that he gave his only begotten Son,
that whosoever believeth in him should not perish,
but have everlasting life.

For God sent not his Son into the world
to condemn the world;
but that the world through him might be saved.

He that believeth on him is not condemned:
but he that believeth not is condemned already,
because he hath not believed
in the name of the only begotten Son of God.

And this is the condemnation,
that light is come into the world,
and men loved darkness rather than light,
because their deeds were evil.

For every one that doeth evil hateth the light,
neither cometh to the light,
lest his deeds should be reproved.

But he that doeth truth cometh to the light,
that his deeds may be made manifest,
that they are wrought in God.

John 3:34-36

For he whom God hath sent speaketh the words of God:
for God giveth not the Spirit by measure unto him.

The Father loveth the Son,
and hath given all things into his hand.

He that believeth on the Son hath everlasting life:
and he that believeth not the Son shall not see life;
but the wrath of God abideth on him.

John 4:21-24

Jesus saith unto her, Woman believe me,
the hour cometh, when ye shall neither in this mountain,
nor yet at Jerusalem, worship the Father.

Ye worship ye know not what: we know what we worship:
for salvation is of the Jews.

But the hour cometh, and now is,
when the true worshippers shall worship the Father
in spirit and in truth:
for the Father seeketh such to worship him.

God is a Spirit: and they that worship him
must worship him in spirit and in truth.

John 8:12

Then spake Jesus again unto them, saying,
I am the light of the world:
he that followeth me shall not walk in darkness,
but shall have the light of life.

John 8:31-32

Then said Jesus to those Jews which believed on him,
If ye continue in my word,
then are ye my disciples indeed;

And ye shall know the truth,
and the truth shall make you free.

John 10:7-11

Then said Jesus unto them again,
Verily, verily, I say unto you,
I am the door of the sheep.

All that ever came before me are thieves and robbers:
but the sheep did not hear them.

I am the door: by me if any man enter in,

he shall be saved,

and shall go in and out, and find pasture.

The thief cometh not,

but for to steal, and to kill, and to destroy:

I am come that they might have life,

and that they might have it more abundantly.

I am the good shepherd:

the good shepherd giveth his life for the sheep.

John 10:27-30

My sheep hear my voice,

and I know them, and they follow me:

And I give unto them eternal life;

and they shall never perish,

neither shall any man pluck them out of my hand.

My Father, which gave them me, is greater than all;

and no man is able to pluck them

out of my Father's hand.

I and my Father are one.

John 12:44-50

Jesus cried and said,
He that believeth on me, believeth not on me,
but on him that sent me.

And he that seeth me seeth him that sent me.

I am come a light into the world,
that whosoever believeth on me
should not abide in darkness.

And if any man hear my words, and believe not,
I judge him not:
for I came not to judge the world,
but to save the world.

He that rejecteth me, and receiveth not my words,
hath one that judgeth him:
the word that I have spoken,
the same shall judge him in the last day.

For I have not spoken of myself;
but the Father which sent me,
he gave me a commandment,
what I should say, and what I should speak.

And I know that his commandment is life everlasting:
whatsoever I speak therefore,
even as the Father said unto me, so I speak.

John 14: 1-6

Let not your heart be troubled:
ye believe in God, believe also in me.

In my Father's house are many mansions:
if it were not so, I would have told you.
I go to prepare a place for you.

And if I go and prepare a place for you, I will come again,
and receive you unto myself;
that where I am, there ye may be also.

And whither I go ye know, and the way ye know.

Thomas saith unto him,
Lord, we know not whither thou goest;
and how can we know the way?

Jesus saith unto him,
I am the way, the truth, and the life:
no man cometh unto the Father, but by me.

John 15

I am the true vine, and my Father is the husbandman.

Every branch in me that beareth not fruit he taketh away:
and every branch that beareth fruit, he purgeth it,
that it may bring forth more fruit.

Now ye are clean through the word
which I have spoken unto you.

Abide in me, and I in you.
As the branch cannot bear fruit of itself,
except it abide in the vine;
no more can ye, except ye abide in me.

I am the vine, ye are the branches:
He that abideth in me, and I in him,
the same bringeth forth much fruit:
for without me ye can do nothing.

If a man abide not in me,
he is cast forth as a branch, and is withered;
and men gather them, and cast them into the fire,
and they are burned.

If ye abide in me, and my words abide in you,
ye shall ask what ye will, and it shall be done unto you.

Herein is my Father glorified, that ye bear much fruit;
so shall ye be my disciples.

As the Father hath loved me, so have I loved you:
continue ye in my love.

If ye keep my commandments, ye shall abide in my love;
even as I have kept my Father's commandments,
and abide in his love.

These things have I spoken unto you,
that my joy might remain in you,
and that your joy might be full.

This is my commandment,
That ye love one another, as I have loved you.

Greater love hath no man than this,
that a man lay down his life for his friends.

Ye are my friends,
if ye do whatsoever I command you.

Henceforth I call you not servants;
for the servant knoweth not what his lord doeth:
but I have called you friends;
for all things that I have heard of my Father
I have made known unto you.

Ye have not chosen me,
but I have chosen you, and ordained you,
that ye should go and bring forth fruit,
and that your fruit should remain:
that whatsoever ye shall ask of the Father in my name,
he may give it you.

These things I command you, that ye love one another.

If the world hate you,
ye know that it hated me before it hated you.

If ye were of the world,
the world would love his own:
but because ye are not of the world,
but I have chosen you out of the world,
therefore the world hateth you.

Remember the word that I said unto you,
The servant is not greater than his lord.
If they have persecuted me,
they will also persecute you;
if they have kept my saying,
they will keep yours also.

But all these things will they do unto you
for my name's sake,
because they know not him that sent me.

If I had not come and spoken unto them,
they had not had sin:
but now they have no cloak for their sin.

He that hateth me hateth my Father also.

If I had not done among them the works
which none other man did,
they had not had sin:
but now have they both seen and hated
both me and my Father.

But this cometh to pass,
that the word might be fulfilled that is written in their law,
They hated me without a cause.

But when the Comforter is come,
whom I will send unto you from the Father,
even the Spirit of truth,
which proceedeth from the Father,
he shall testify of me:

And ye also shall bear witness,
because ye have been with me from the beginning.

John 16:32-33

Behold, the hour cometh, yea, is now come,
that ye shall be scattered, every man to his own,
and shall leave me alone:
and yet I am not alone,
because the Father is with me.

These things I have spoken unto you,
that in me ye might have peace.
In the world ye shall have tribulation:
but be of good cheer;
I have overcome the world.

John 17

These words spake Jesus,
and lifted up his eyes to heaven, and said,
Father, the hour is come; glorify thy Son,
that thy Son also may glorify thee:

As thou hast given him power over all flesh,
that he should give eternal life
to as many as thou hast given him.

And this is life eternal,
that they might know thee the only true God,
and Jesus Christ, whom thou hast sent.

I have glorified thee on the earth:
I have finished the work which thou gavest me to do.

And now, O Father, glorify thou me with thine own self
with the glory which I had with thee
before the world was.

I have manifested thy name unto the men
which thou gavest me out of the world:
thine they were, and thou gavest them me;
and they have kept thy word.

Now they have known that all things
whatsoever thou hast given me are of thee.

For I have given unto them the words
which thou gavest me;
and they have received them,
and have known surely that I came out from thee,
and they have believed that thou didst send me.

I pray for them: I pray not for the world,
but for them which thou hast given me; for they are thine.

And all mine are thine, and thine are mine;
and I am glorified in them.

And now I am no more in the world,
but these are in the world, and I come to thee.
Holy Father, keep through thine own name
those whom thou hast given me,
that they may be one, as we are.

While I was with them in the world,
I kept them in thy name:
those that thou gavest me I have kept,
and none of them is lost, but the son of perdition;
that the scripture might be fulfilled.

And now come I to thee;
and these things I speak in the world,
that they might have my joy fulfilled in themselves.

I have given them thy word; and the world hath hated them,
because they are not of the world,
even as I am not of the world.

I pray not that thou shouldest take them out of the world,
but that thou shouldest keep them from the evil.

They are not of the world, even as I am not of the world.

Sanctify them through thy truth: thy word is truth.

As thou hast sent me into the world,
even so have I also sent them into the world.

And for their sakes I sanctify myself,
that they also might be sanctified through the truth.

Neither pray I for these alone,
but for them also which shall believe on me
through their word;

That they all may be one;
as thou, Father, art in me, and I in thee,
that they also may be one in us:
that the world may believe that thou hast sent me.

And the glory which thou gavest me I have given them;
that they may be one, even as we are one:

I in them, and thou in me,
that they may be made perfect in one;
and that the world may know that thou hast sent me,
and hast loved them, as thou hast loved me.

Father, I will that they also, whom thou hast given me,
be with me where I am;
that they may behold my glory, which thou hast given me:
for thou lovedst me before the foundation of the world.

O righteous Father, the world hath not known thee:
but I have known thee,
and these have known that thou hast sent me.

And I have declared unto them thy name, and will declare it:
that the love wherewith thou hast loved me
may be in them, and I in them.

John 18:33-38

Then Pilate entered into the judgment hall again,
and called Jesus, and said unto him,
Art thou the King of the Jews?

Jesus answered him,
Sayest thou this thing of thyself,
or did others tell it thee of me?

Pilate answered, Am I a Jew?
Thine own nation and the chief priests
have delivered thee unto me:
what hast thou done?

Jesus answered,
My kingdom is not of this world:
if my kingdom were of this world,
then would my servants fight,
that I should not be delivered to the Jews:
but now is my kingdom not from hence.

Pilate therefore said unto him,
Art thou a king then?
Jesus answered,
Thou sayest that I am a king.

To this end was I born,
and for this cause came I into the world,
that I should bear witness unto the truth.
Every one that is of the truth heareth my voice.

Pilate saith unto him, What is truth?
And when he had said this,
he went out again unto the Jews,
and saith unto them,
I find in him no fault at all.

Romans

Romans 1:16-32

For I am not ashamed of the gospel of Christ:
    for it is the power of God unto salvation
to every one that believeth;
to the Jew first, and also to the Greek.

For therein is the righteousness of God
revealed from faith to faith: as it is written,
The just shall live by faith.

For the wrath of God is revealed from heaven
against all ungodliness and unrighteousness of men,
who hold the truth in unrighteousness;

Because that which may be known of God is manifest in them;
for God hath shewed it unto them.

For the invisible things of him
from the creation of the world are clearly seen,
being understood by the things that are made,
even his eternal power and Godhead;
so that they are without excuse:

Because that, when they knew God,
they glorified him not as God, neither were thankful;
but became vain in their imaginations,
and their foolish heart was darkened.

Professing themselves to be wise, they became fools,

And changed the glory of the uncorruptible God
into an image made like to corruptible man,
and to birds, and fourfooted beasts, and creeping things.

Wherefore God also gave them up to uncleanesss
through the lusts of their own hearts,
to dishonour their own bodies between themselves:

Who changed the truth of God into a lie,
and worshipped and served the creature
more than the Creator, who is blessed for ever. Amen.

For this cause God gave them up unto vile affections:
for even their women did change the natural use
into that which is against nature:

And likewise also the men,
leaving the natural use of the woman,
burned in their lust one toward another;
men with men working that which is unseemly,
and receiving in themselves that recompence
of their error which was meet.

And even as they did not like to retain God in their knowledge,
God gave them over to a reprobate mind,
to do those things which are not convenient;

Being filled with all unrighteousness, fornication,
wickedness, covetousness, maliciousness;
full of envy, murder, debate,
deceit, malignity; whisperers,

Backbiters, haters of God, despiteful,
proud, boasters, inventors of evil things,
disobedient to parents,

Without understanding, covenant-breakers,
without natural affection, implacable, unmerciful:

Who knowing the judgment of God,
that they which commit such things are worthy of death,
not only do the same,
but have pleasure in them that do them.

Romans 2:11-16

For there is no respect of persons with God.

For as many as have sinned without law
shall also perish without law:
and as many as have sinned in the law
shall be judged by the law;

(For not the hearers of the law are just before God,
but the doers of the law shall be justified.

For when the Gentiles, which have not the law,
do by nature the things contained in the law,
these, having not the law, are a law unto themselves:

Which shew the work of the law written in their hearts,
their conscience also bearing witness, and their thoughts
the mean while accusing or else excusing one another;)

In the day when God shall judge the secrets of men
by Jesus Christ according to my gospel.

Romans 3:19-31

N ow we know that what things soever the law saith,
it saith to them who are under the law:
that every mouth may be stopped,
and all the world may become guilty before God.

Therefore by the deeds of the law
there shall no flesh be justified in his sight:
for by the law is the knowledge of sin.

But now the righteousness of God
without the law is manifested,
being witnessed by the law and the prophets;

Even the righteousness of God
which is by faith of Jesus Christ
unto all and upon all them that believe:
for there is no difference:

For all have sinned, and come short of the glory of God;

Being justified freely by his grace
through the redemption that is in Christ Jesus:

Whom God hath set forth to be a propitiation
through faith in his blood,
to declare his righteousness for remission of sins
that are past,
through the forbearance of God;

To declare, I say, at this time his righteousness:
that he might be just,
and the justifier of him which believeth in Jesus.

Where is boasting then? It is excluded.
By what law? of works?
Nay: but by the law of faith.

Therefore we conclude that a man is justified by faith
without the deeds of the law.

Is he the God of the Jews only?
is he not also of the Gentiles? Yes, of the Gentiles also:

Seeing it is one God,

which shall justify the circumcision by faith,

and the uncircumcision through faith.

Do we then make void the law through faith?

God forbid: yea, we establish the law.

Romans 6:23

For the wages of sin is death;

but the gift of God is eternal life

through Jesus Christ our Lord.

Romans 8:28-39

And we know that all things work together for good
to them that love God,

to them who are the called according to his purpose.

For whom he did foreknow,

he also did predestinate to be conformed

to the image of his Son,

that he might be the firstborn among many brethren.

Moreover whom he did predestinate, them he also called:

and whom he called, them he also justified:

and whom he justified, them he also glorified.

What shall we then say to these things?

If God be for us, who can be against us?

He that spared not his own Son,

but delivered him up for us all,

how shall he not with him also freely give us all things?

Who shall lay any thing to the charge of God's elect?

It is God that justifieth.

Who is he that condemneth?

It is Christ that died, yea rather, that is risen again,

who is even at the right hand of God,

who also maketh intercession for us.

Who shall separate us from the love of Christ?

shall tribulation, or distress, or persecution,

or famine, or nakedness, or peril, or sword?

As it is written,

For thy sake we are killed all the day long;

we are accounted as sheep for the slaughter.

Nay, in all these things we are more than conquerors
through him that loved us.

For I am persuaded, that neither death, nor life,
nor angels, nor principalities, nor powers,
nor things present, nor things to come,

Nor height, nor depth, nor any other creature,
shall be able to separate us from the love of God,
which is in Christ Jesus our Lord.

1 Corinthians

1 Cor. 1:17-31

For Christ sent me not to baptize,
  but to preach the gospel:
not with wisdom of words,
lest the cross of Christ should be made of none effect.

For the preaching of the cross
is to them that perish foolishness;
but unto us which are saved it is the power of God.

For it is written, I will destroy the wisdom of the wise,
and will bring to nothing
the understanding of the prudent.

Where is the wise? where is the scribe?
where is the disputer of this world?
hath not God made foolish the wisdom of this world?

For after that in the wisdom of God
the world by wisdom knew not God,
it pleased God by the foolishness of preaching
to save them that believe.

For the Jews require a sign,
and the Greeks seek after wisdom:

But we preach Christ crucified,
unto the Jews a stumblingblock,
and unto the Greeks foolishness;

But unto them which are called,
both Jews and Greeks,
Christ the power of God, and the wisdom of God.

Because the foolishness of God is wiser than men;
and the weakness of God is stronger than men.

For ye see your calling, brethren,
how that not many wise men after the flesh,
not many mighty, not many noble, are called:

But God hath chosen the foolish things of the world
to confound the wise;
and God hath chosen the weak things of the world
to confound the things which are mighty;

And base things of the world,
and things which are despised,
hath God chosen, yea, and things which are not,
to bring to nought things that are:

That no flesh should glory in his presence.

But of him are ye in Christ Jesus,
who of God is made unto us wisdom,
and righteousness, and sanctification,
and redemption:

That, according as it is written,
He that glorieth, let him glory in the Lord.

1 Cor. 2

And I, brethren, when I came to you,
came not with excellency of speech or of wisdom,
declaring unto you the testimony of God.

For I determined not to know any thing among you,
save Jesus Christ, and him crucified.

And I was with you in weakness, and in fear,
and in much trembling.

And my speech and my preaching
was not with enticing words of man's wisdom,
but in demonstration of the Spirit and of power:

That your faith should not stand in the wisdom of men,
but in the power of God.

Howbeit we speak wisdom among them that are perfect:
yet not the wisdom of this world,
nor of the princes of this world,
that come to nought:

But we speak the wisdom of God in a mystery,
even the hidden wisdom,
which God ordained before the world unto our glory:

Which none of the princes of this world knew:
for had they known it,
they would not have crucified the Lord of glory.

But as it is written, Eye hath not seen, nor ear heard,
neither have entered into the heart of man,
the things which God hath prepared for them that love him.

But God hath revealed them unto us by his Spirit:
for the Spirit searcheth all things,
yea, the deep things of God.

For what man knoweth the things of a man,
save the spirit of man which is in him?
even so the things of God knoweth no man,
but the Spirit of God.

Now we have received, not the spirit of the world,
but the spirit which is of God;
that we might know the things
that are freely given to us of God.

Which things also we speak,
not in the words which man's wisdom teacheth,
but which the Holy Ghost teacheth;
comparing spiritual things with spiritual.

But the natural man receiveth not
the things of the Spirit of God:
for they are foolishness unto him:
neither can he know them,
because they are spiritually discerned.

But he that is spiritual judgeth all things,
yet he himself is judged of no man.

For who hath known the mind of the Lord,
that he may instruct him?
But we have the mind of Christ.

1 Cor. 3:16-23

Know ye not that ye are the temple of God,
and that the Spirit of God dwelleth in you?

If any man defile the temple of God,
him shall God destroy;
for the temple of God is holy, which temple ye are.

Let no man deceive himself.
If any man among you seemth to be wise in this world,
let him become a fool, that he may be wise.

For the wisdom of this world is foolishness with God.
For it is written,
He taketh the wise in their own craftiness.

And again,
The Lord knoweth the thoughts of the wise,
that they are vain.

Therefore let no man glory in men.
For all things are yours;

Whether Paul, or Apollos, or Cephas, or the world,
or life, or death, or things present, or things to come;
all are yours;

And ye are Christ's; and Christ is God's.

1 Cor. 4:20

For the kingdom of God is not in word, but in power.

1 Cor. 13

Though I speak with the tongues of men and of angels,
and have not charity*,   *(love)
I am become as sounding brass, or a tinkling cymbal.

And though I have the gift of prophecy,
and understand all mysteries, and all knowledge;
and though I have all faith,
so that I could remove mountains,
and have not charity, I am nothing.

And though I bestow all my goods to feed the poor,
and though I give my body to be burned,
and have not charity,
it profiteth me nothing.

Charity suffereth long, and is kind;
charity envieth not;
charity vaunteth not itself, is not puffed up.

Doth not behave itself unseemly,
seekth not her own,
is not easily provoked, thinketh no evil;

Rejoiceth not in iniquity, but rejoiceth in the truth;

Beareth all things, believeth all things,
hopeth all things, endureth all things.

Charity never faileth:
but whether there be prophecies, they shall fail;
whether there be tongues, they shall cease;
whether there be knowledge, it shall vanish away.

For we know in part, and we prophesy in part.

But when that which is perfect is come,
then that which is in part shall be done away.

When I was a child, I spake as a child,
I understood as a child, I thought as a child:
but when I became a man, I put away childish things.

For now we see through a glass,
darkly; but then face to face:
now I know in part;
but then shall I know even as also I am known.

And now abideth faith, hope, charity, these three;
but the greatest of these is charity.

charity* (love) - The Greek word here is *agape*. It is defined as the highest form of
love, like the divine love that God has for mankind. *Agape* is often translated as
"love" in the KJV, most notably in John 3:16. For this reason, I choose to simply say
"love" wherever I see "charity" in these verses.

Galatians

Galatians 5:22-26

But the fruit of the Spirit is love, joy, peace, longsuffering, gentleness, goodness, faith,

Meekness, temperance: against such there is no law.

And they that are Christ's have crucified the flesh with the affections and lusts.

If we live in the Spirit, let us also walk in the Spirit.

Let us not be desirous of vain glory, provoking one another, envying one another.

Galatians 6:7-8

Be not deceived; God is not mocked: for whatsoever a man soweth, that shall he also reap.

For he that soweth to his flesh shall of the flesh reap corruption; but he that soweth to the Spirit
shall of the Spirit reap live everlasting.

Ephesians

Ephesians 6:10-17

Finally, my brethren, be strong in the Lord,
and in the power of his might.

Put on the whole armour of God,
that ye may be able to stand against the wiles of the devil.

For we wrestle not against flesh and blood,
but against principalities, against powers,
against the rulers of the darkness of this world,
against spiritual wickedness in high places.

Wherefore take unto you the whole armour of God,
that ye may be able to withstand in the evil day,
and having done all, to stand.

Stand therefore,
having your loins girt about with truth,
and having on the breastplate of righteousness;

And your feet shod with the preparation
of the gospel of peace;

Above all, taking the shield of faith,
wherewith ye shall be able to quench
all the fiery darts of the wicked.

And take the helmet of salvation,
and the sword of the Spirit,
which is the word of God:

1 Timothy

1 Timothy 6:7-12

For we brought nothing into this world,
and it is certain we can carry nothing out.

And having food and raiment let us be therewith content.

But they that will be rich fall into temptation and a snare,
and into many foolish and hurtful lusts,
which drown men in destruction and perdition.

For the love of money is the root of all evil:
which while some coveted after,
they have erred from the faith,
and pierced themselves through with many sorrows.

But thou, O man of God, flee these things;
and follow after righteousness, godliness,
faith, love, patience, meekness.

Fight the good fight of faith, lay hold on eternal life, whereunto thou art also called, and hast professed a good profession before many witnesses.

2 Timothy

2 Timothy 3:16-17

All scripture is given by inspiration of God,
and is profitable for doctrine, for reproof,
for correction, for instruction in righteousness:

That the man of God may be perfect,
throughly furnished unto all good works.

Hebrews

Hebrews 4:12-16

For the word of God is quick, and powerful,
and sharper than any two-edged sword,
piercing even to the dividing asunder
of soul and spirit, and of the joints and marrow,
and is a discerner
of the thoughts and intents of the heart.

Neither is there any creature
that is not manifest in his sight:
but all things are naked and opened
unto the eyes of him
with whom we have to do.

Seeing then that we have a great high priest,
that is passed into the heavens,

Jesus the Son of God,
let us hold fast our profession.

For we have not an high priest
which cannot be touched
with the feeling of our infirmities;
but was in all points tempted
like as we are, yet without sin.

Let us therefore come boldly
unto the throne of grace,
that we may obtain mercy,
and find grace to help in time of need.

Hebrews 11:1

Now faith is the substance of things hoped for,
the evidence of things not seen.

Hebrews 11:6

But without faith it is impossible to please him;
for he that cometh to God must believe that he is,
and that he is a rewarder of them that diligently seek him.

James

James 2:17-26

Even so faith, if it hath not works, is dead, being alone.

Yea, a man may say, Thou hast faith, and I have works:
shew me thy faith without thy works,
and I will shew thee my faith by my works.

Thou believest that there is one God; thou doest well:
the devils also believe, and tremble.

But wilt thou know, O vain man,
that faith without works is dead?

Was not Abraham our father justified by works,
when he had offered Isaac his son upon the altar?

Seest thou how faith wrought with his works,
and by works was faith made perfect?

And the scripture was fulfilled which saith,
Abraham believed God,
and it was imputed unto him for righteousness:
and he was called the Friend of God.

Ye see then how that by works a man is justified,
and not by faith only.

Likewise also was not Rahab the harlot
justified by works, when she had received the messengers,
and had sent them out another way?

For as the body without the spirit is dead,
so faith without works is dead also.

1 John

1 John 1

That which was from the beginning,
which we have heard,
which we have seen with our eyes,
which we have looked upon,
and our hands have handled, of the Word of life;

(For the life was manifested, and we have seen it,
and bear witness, and shew unto you that eternal life,
which was with the Father, and was manifested unto us;)

That which we have seen and heard declare we unto you,
that ye also may have fellowship with us:
and truly our fellowship is with the Father,
and with his Son Jesus Christ.

And these things write we unto you,
that your joy may be full.

This then is the message which we have heard of him,
and declare unto you,
that God is light, and in him is no darkness at all.

If we say that we have fellowship with him,
and walk in darkness,
we lie, and do not the truth:

But if we walk in the light, as he is in the light,
we have fellowship one with another,
and the blood of Jesus Christ his Son cleanseth us from all sin.

If we say that we have no sin, we deceive ourselves,
and the truth is not in us.

If we confess our sins,
he is faithful and just to forgive us our sins,
and to cleanse us from all unrighteousness.

If we say that we have not sinned,
we make him a liar, and his word is not in us.

1 John 4

B eloved, believe not every spirit,
　　but try the spirits whether they are of God:
because many false prophets are gone out into the world.

Hereby know ye the Spirit of God:
Every spirit that confesseth
that Jesus Christ is come in the flesh is of God:

And every spirit that confesseth not
that Jesus Christ is come in the flesh is not of God:
and this is that spirit of anti-christ,
whereof ye have heard that it should come;
and even now already is it in the world.

Ye are of God, little children, and have overcome them:
because greater is he that is in you,
than he that is in the world.

They are of the world: therefore speak they of the world,
and the world heareth them.

We are of God: he that knowth God heareth us;
he that is not of God heareth not us.
Hereby know we the spirit of truth, and the spirit of error.

Beloved, let us love one another:

for love is of God;

and every one that loveth is born of God, and knoweth God.

He that loveth not knoweth not God;

for God is love.

In this was manifested the love of God toward us,

because that God sent his only begotten Son into the world,

that we might live through him.

Herein is love, not that we loved God,

but that he loved us,

and sent his Son to be the propitiation for our sins.

Beloved, if God so loved us,

we ought also to love one another.

No man hath seen God at any time.

If we love one another, God dwelleth in us,

and his love is perfected in us.

Hereby know we that we dwell in him, and he in us,

because he hath given us of his Spirit.

And we have seen and do testify
that the Father sent the Son to be the Saviour of the world.

Whosoever shall confess that Jesus is the Son of God,
God dwelleth in him, and he in God.

And we have known and believed
the love that God hath to us.
God is love; and he that dwelleth in love dwelleth in God,
and God in him.

Herein is our love made perfect,
that we may have boldness in the day of judgment:
because as he is, so are we in this world.

There is no fear in love;
but perfect love casteth out fear:
because fear hath torment.
He that feareth is not made perfect in love.

We love him, because he first loved us.

If a man say, I love God, and hateth his brother,
he is a liar:
for he that loveth not his brother whom he hath seen,
how can he love God whom he hath not seen?

And this commandment have we from him,
That he who loveth God love his brother also.

1 John 5 1:5

Whosoever believeth that Jesus is the Christ
is born of God:
and every one that loveth him that begat
loveth him also that is begotten of him.

By this we know that we love the children of God,
when we love God, and keep his commandments.

For this is the love of God,
that we keep his commandments:
and his commandments are not grievous.

For whatsoever is born of God overcometh the world:
and this is the victory that overcometh the world,
even our faith.

Who is he that overcometh the world,
but he that believeth that Jesus is the Son of God?

To order additional copies of this book or other books by Tzyon Press go to:

www.howtomemorizethebible.com